Competing with the Government
the Government

Anticompetitive Behavior
and
Public Enterprises

Competing with the Government

Anticompetitive Behavior and Public Enterprises

EDITED BY
R. Richard Geddes

CONTRIBUTING AUTHORS
R. Richard Geddes
David E. M. Sappington
J. Gregory Sidak
Peter J. Wallison

HOOVER INSTITUTION PRESS
Stanford University   Stanford, California

The Hoover Institution on War, Revolution and Peace,
founded at Stanford University in 1919 by Herbert Hoover,
who went on to become the thirty-first president of
the United States, is an interdisciplinary research center
for advanced study on domestic and international affairs.
The views expressed in its publications are entirely those of
the authors and do not necessarily reflect the views of the staff,
officers, or Board of Overseers of the Hoover Institution.

www.hoover.org

Hoover Institution Press Publication No. 523

Copyright © 2004 by the Board of Trustees of the
   Leland Stanford Junior University
All rights reserved. No part of this publication may be reproduced,
stored in a retrieval system, or transmitted in any form or by any
means, electronic, mechanical, photocopying, recording, or otherwise,
without written permission of the publisher.

First printing, 2004
11   10   09   08   07   06   05   04   9   8   7   6   5   4   3   2   1

Manufactured in the United States of America

The paper used in this publication meets the minimum requirements
of the American National Standard for Information Sciences—Permanence
of Paper for Printed Library Materials, ANSI Z39.48–1992.

Library of Congress Cataloging-in-Publication Data
Competing with the government : anticompetitive behavior and public
enterprises / edited by R. Richard Geddes.
      p.   cm.— (Hoover Institution Press publication ; 523)
Includes bibliographical references and index.
ISBN 0-8179-3992-X (alk. paper)
1. Government business enterprises—United States.   2. Corporations,
Government—United States.   3. Government monopolies—United States.
4. Competition, Unfair—United States.   5. Antitrust law—United States.
I. Geddes, R. Richard.   II. Series.
HD3885.C66   2004
338.6′048′0973—dc22   2003025450

Contents

Contributors

R. RICHARD GEDDES is associate professor in the Department of Policy Analysis and Management at Cornell University. He holds PhD and MA degrees in economics from the University of Chicago. His written work has appeared in the *American Economic Review*, the *Journal of Regulatory Economics*, the *Encyclopedia of Law and Economics*, the *Journal of Legal Studies*, the *Journal of Law, Economics, and Organization*, and the *Journal of Law and Economics*. He was a Visiting Faculty Fellow at Yale Law School in 1995–1996 and a National Fellow at the Hoover Institution in 1999–2000. He is an adjunct scholar of the American Enterprise Institute.

DAVID E. M. SAPPINGTON holds the Lanzillotti-McKethan Eminent Scholar Chair in the Department of Economics at the University of Florida. He also serves as director of the University's Public Policy Research Center. Until recently, he was the Chief Economist at the Federal Communications Commission. Professor Sappington has written widely on numerous regulatory issues and is the author of two books and more than 80 articles published in leading economics journals. He has served on the editorial boards of several academic journals.

J. GREGORY SIDAK studies regulatory and antitrust policy concerning network industries. He is the F. K. Weyerhaeuser Fellow in Law and Economics Emeritus at the American Enterprise Institute and president and chief executive officer of Criterion Economics, L.L.C., an economic consulting firm based in Washington, D.C. Mr. Sidak served as deputy general counsel of the Federal Communications Commission from 1987 to 1989 and as senior counsel and economist to the Council of Economic Advisers in the Executive Office of the President from 1986 to 1987. He has written on a wide variety of regulatory and legal issues.

PETER J. WALLISON is a resident fellow at the American Enterprise Institute (AEI) and codirector of AEI's program on Financial Market Deregulation. He is an expert on financial services and banking law and has written widely in those areas. Before joining AEI, Mr. Wallison practiced at Gibson, Dunn & Crutcher in Washington, D.C. From June 1981 to January 1985, he was general counsel of the U.S. Treasury Department. During 1986 and 1987, he was counsel to the president of the United States.

Introduction

The Issues

Government-owned and government-subsidized firms in the United States compete with private firms in a wide variety of activities. Amtrak carried freight on the back of its passenger trains. Government-owned electric utilities, such as the Tennessee Valley Authority, compete directly with private firms in the provision of electricity. TVA has also considered expanding into cable television and telecommunications. City governments built waterworks to compete directly with private providers. Fannie Mae and Freddie Mac compete with private firms in automated underwriting systems. The National Weather Service competes with private firms in the provision of customized weather forecasts. The U.S. Postal Service provides both package and express mail delivery in direct competition with private rivals. The Coast Guard competed with private firms in nonemergency marine assistance, and so on. Competition between government and private firms is even more important overseas, where many countries historically have had greater government involvement in economic activity.

Competition between government and private firms is disconcerting. Government firms are often endowed with government-granted privileges and immunities not enjoyed by private rivals. Those benefits may include monopoly power, credit guarantees, freedom from paying investors an expected rate of return, exemption from bankruptcy, tax exemptions, direct subsidies, and immunity from antitrust prosecution, disclosure requirements, and other regulations. All such privileges and immunities are valuable.

Those privileges give government firms an artificial competitive advantage over private rivals. By artificial, I mean that a government firm's competitive advantage is not based on economic factors such as superior management skills, more efficient technology, enhanced innovation, better labor relations, better corporate governance, or harder work. The firm's competitive advantage is an artifact of its government-granted benefits.

Government firms may use their special benefits in anticompetitive ways. For example, they might use their monopoly power and other advantages to sustain prices below true economic cost in markets where they face competition. Or they might use those privileges to raise rivals' costs or preclude rivals from entering other markets. They might also leverage their monopoly power in one market into other, formerly competitive markets or engage in a variety of other anticompetitive actions.

Anticompetitive behavior by government firms is harmful. First, there is a straightforward misallocation of resources because prices are not in alignment with true economic cost. Because they are not as concerned with profits as their private counterparts, government-owned firms are more willing to set price below cost and keep it there without regard to long-term losses. Second, more efficient but unsubsidized private firms will contract, not invest, or may not start up if they observe or anticipate competition from a government rival. Third, if there is uncertainty over a government firm's intention or ability to expand into an activity, that uncertainty will contribute to private disinvestment. Fourth, taxpayers or other captive groups will have to fund more (or all) of the overhead costs in the competitive activity, even though customers using the good or service are willing to pay for it. Finally, ventures outside of a government firm's core activity may divert resources from that core, socially beneficial activity.

Although competition between government and private firms is an important economic phenomenon, academic research addressing the topic is limited. Scholars have instead tended to focus on the behavior of privately owned firms. Nor is there a developed body of law in the United States on this subject. Antitrust law has focused almost exclusively on competion among privately owned firms. The essays in this book attempt to address that gap.

In Chapter 1, David Sappington and Gregory Sidak discuss the objectives of state-owned enterprises (SOEs). They find that SOEs are concerned about profits as well as the scale and scope of their operations. They explore the implications of such a firm acting to maximize both its size and profits and find that an SOE is more likely to engage in anticompetitive behavior than is a pure profit maximizer. They show that an SOE is more willing to price competitive products below cost than is a privately owned firm, even if the SOE lacks predatory intent. They go on to show that an SOE has an extra incentive to engage in a variety of activities that expand its revenue, including relaxation of regulatory constraints, raising rivals' costs, and erecting entry barriers for rivals. They conclude by showing that, in addition to the incentive, an SOE has enhanced ability to undertake those activities.

In Chapter 2, I review a variety of instances in which SOEs and private firms compete, suggesting that such competition is more common in the United States than generally thought. I discuss why anticompetitive behavior by SOEs is likely to be socially harmful and review the wide array of government-granted privileges and immunities typically enjoyed by SOEs and ways in which they might be used anticompetitively. I then present seven case studies of industries in which government and private firms either currently or historically have competed in the United States. These include freight carriage, water utilities, financial services, electric utilities, information provision, weather forecasting, and marine-towing services.

Chapters 1 and 2 together demonstrate that SOEs have the incentive, the opportunity, and the capacity to inefficiently compete with private firms. The remaining chapters illustrate that they will, in fact, engage in anticompetitive behavior.

In Chapter 3, Peter Wallison examines anticompetitive behavior by government-sponsored enterprises (GSEs), specifically Fannie Mae and Freddie Mac. He catalogs the advantages those firms have as a result of their government sponsorship. He then applies to the GSEs and their attempted monopolization of the automated underwriting market and other mortgage finance–related markets the analysis of the 2001 decision by the Court of Appeals for the D.C. Circuit in the Microsoft case. Using the analysis in the decision as a road map, he finds that a strong case can be made that the GSEs violated Section 2 of the Sherman Act by monopolizing the automated underwriting market.

In Chapter 4, I consider anticompetitive behavior in postal services in the United States and abroad. Postal services are of particular interest because of both their size and the level of government involvement in almost all countries and because they usually compete directly with private firms in several markets. I first examine the case of the U.S. Postal Service (USPS) and briefly review the special government-granted privileges, subsidies, and immunities enjoyed by the USPS. Using the changes instituted by the 1970 Postal Reorganization Act as a test, I present data consistent with anticompetitive behavior by the U.S. Postal Service. I then review examples of anticompetitive behavior that have arisen in postal services in other countries.

This topic raises fundamental questions about the proper relationship between business and government in a market economy. Should government operate where private business is actively providing a good or service? If, over time, private enterprise expands the scope of activities it provides, does government have a duty to reduce the activities it provides? If government and private firms do compete, should government firms be able to use their array of privileges and immunities to outbid private rivals in the marketplace?

Collectively, the essays in this book suggest a need for significant policy change regarding competition between government and private firms in the United States. At a minimum, enhanced scrutiny of SOEs and GSEs under antitrust law is appropriate. Additionally, it may be wise to construe narrowly any statutory monopoly that is conferred on an SOE and to limit strictly its ability to expand beyond the market covered by that monopoly.

Acknowledgments

I am grateful to John Raisian and Richard Sousa for their support and encouragement on this project. I am also grateful to the Hoover Institution for financial and editorial support in the preparation of this book.

Chapter 1

Anticompetitive Behavior by State-Owned Enterprises: Incentives and Capabilities

David E. M. Sappington
and
J. Gregory Sidak

State-owned enterprises (SOEs), also known as public enterprises, are owned by governments rather than private investors and compete directly with private, profit-maximizing enterprises in many important markets. For example, government postal firms typically offer overnight mail and package shipping services in direct competition with private delivery companies. In addition, many public hospitals and educational institutions compete directly with private suppliers of similar services.

Production by public enterprises is particularly widespread in developing countries. During the 1980s, for example, public enterprises accounted for approximately 14 percent of gross domestic product in African nations and approximately 11 percent in developing countries as a whole.[1]

Typically, SOEs are required to pursue goals other than pure profit maximization. One might therefore suspect they would act less aggressively toward their competitors than would private, profit-maximizing firms. We show, however, that the opposite is often the case. Even though they may be less concerned with generating profit, SOEs have stronger incentives than profit-maximizing firms to pursue activities that disadvantage competitors. Furthermore, such incentives can become more pronounced as an SOE's concern with profit becomes less pronounced. Potential activities to disadvantage competitors include setting prices below cost, misstating costs and choosing inefficient technologies to circumvent restrictions on below-cost pricing, raising the operating costs of existing rivals, and erecting entry barriers to preclude the operation of new competitors.

The increased incentive of SOEs to disadvantage competitors can arise from governmental policy objectives and other forces that induce SOEs to value an expanded operating scale for its own sake. To illustrate, SOEs are often instructed to increase local employment and/or to ensure that affordable service is provided ubiquitously to low income families. Such directives blunt incentives for profit maximization and thereby introduce a system in which the success of an SOE manager is measured more by the scale and scope of operations than by the profit those operations generate. Under such an explicit or implicit reward structure, SOEs act as if they value expanded scale and scope—as proxied by revenue, for example—as well as, or instead of, profit. The enhanced value placed on revenue or output leads the SOE to undertake aggressive actions in pursuit of expanded output and revenue, including anticompetitive behavior against private, profit-maximizing enterprises.[2]

In this chapter, we first provide some background on competition law and its application to SOEs.[3] We then explain in detail why, contrary to the prevailing view, SOEs have particularly strong incentives to act anticompetitively. Finally, we explain why SOEs also may have enhanced ability to act on those incentives.

Some Legal Background

For more than a century after the passage of the Sherman Act, the United States led the world in developing a body of legal and economic principles for analyzing anticompetitive behavior by private enterprises. The U.S. Constitution, however, is thought to immunize from U.S. antitrust law much anticompetitive behavior by SOEs. Within the American federalist system, the Supreme Court has long addressed whether states may impose and supervise policies that reduce competition. Those cases articulate the state-action immunity in U.S. antitrust law, which generously immunizes states (and, less generously, municipalities) from antitrust claims as long as they actively supervise the suppression of competition. The crude rule of thumb is that private plaintiffs suing states for anticompetitive behavior generally lose.

The body of law with respect to federal government activities that impair competition is far less developed. If a federal SOE cloaks itself with the claim of sovereign immunity and if Congress has not consented to claims against the sovereign, including the sovereign's economic enterprises, a plaintiff generally has little chance to prevail in an antitrust proceeding against the SOE. So it is not surprising that the antitrust jurisprudence on SOEs pales in comparison to American antitrust precedent on most business practices.

Capitalism itself has also contributed to the stunted growth of American case law on SOEs. Unlike Europe, Australia, New Zealand, or even Canada, the United States has never embraced government ownership of enterprise. Railroads, telephone companies, electric utilities, banks, airlines, steel mills, automobile factories, and aircraft plants have routinely been owned and operated by the state in Europe and much of the world.[4] In contrast, the U.S. government generally has refrained from nationalizing and from directly managing private industries except in wartime.

Times have changed. The United States now feels the growing influence of the European Commission (EC) and various national enforcement agencies around the world, as General Electric's failed acquisition of Honeywell in 2001 attests.[5] Less noticed than the defeat of the GE-Honeywell merger, but equally important for its long-term implications for the development of competition law on all continents, was the EC's decision in 2001 regarding Deutsche Post AG, the German postal monopoly now undergoing privatization.

The EC found that Deutsche Post used profits from its state-granted monopoly in letter mail services to subsidize efforts to dominate the parcel delivery business in Germany by pricing below cost and undercutting competitors.[6] The EC ordered Deutsche Post to divest its parcel delivery business and to engage the new owner only on an arms'-length basis for any continuing commercial relationships.

The *Deutsche Post* case could soon become relevant to SOEs owned by the U.S. government. In 2002, the U.S. Court of Appeals for the Ninth Circuit held in the *Flamingo Industries* case that the Postal Service was subject to federal antitrust law because "Congress has withdrawn the cloak of sovereign immunity from the Postal Service and given it the status of a private corporation."[7] The Ninth Circuit found that the Postal Service lost its sovereign status upon enactment of the Postal Reorganization Act of 1970, which provided that "The Postal Service shall have the . . . power to sue and be sued in its official name."[8]

Another significant development concerning competition law for SOEs is the complaint filed by United Parcel Service in 2000 against Canada Post under Chapter 11 of the North American Free Trade Agreement (NAFTA).[9] Chapter 11 permits an investor of one signatory nation to initiate arbitration against another signatory nation for its failure to comply with NAFTA's obligations concerning foreign investment and regulation of monopolies. Chapter 11 enables a foreign firm to sue for damages caused by a nation's preferential treatment of its SOE, even though sovereign immunity might block an analytically identical case brought by a citizen of that same nation and styled as a violation of its domestic law. The applicable law is not necessarily that of any NAFTA country.

The *Flamingo Industries* decision and the pending *Canada Post* NAFTA arbitration illustrate how American SOEs such as the U.S.

Postal Service, the Tennessee Valley Authority, and Federal Prison Industries all could become the targets of analogous NAFTA complaints filed by Canadian or Mexican parties under NAFTA, as well as targets of antitrust suits filed by American plaintiffs under American law.

Anticompetitive Incentives of State-Owned Enterprises

In this section, we explain why SOEs have stronger incentives than private firms to engage in anticompetitive activities. We demonstrate that when an SOE values an expanded scale of operation in addition to profit, it will be less concerned than its private, profit-maximizing counterpart with the extra costs associated with increased output. Consequently, even though an SOE may value the profit its anticompetitive activities can generate less highly than does a private profit-maximizing firm, the SOE will still pursue anticompetitive activities that expand its own output and revenue. To illustrate, the SOE might set the price it charges for a product below its marginal cost of production, particularly if the product is one for which demand increases substantially as price declines.[10] If prohibitions on below-cost pricing are in effect, an SOE will have a strong incentive to understate its marginal cost of production or to overinvest in fixed operating costs to reduce variable operating costs. A public enterprise may also be more inclined than a private, profit-maximizing firm to raise its rivals' costs and to undertake activities designed to exclude competitors from the market because those activities expand the scale and scope of the SOE's operations.

The Objective of an SOE

Different SOEs often have different assigned missions and different goals. For example, the U.S. Postal Service is charged with providing ubiquitous service throughout the United States at uniform rates across different geographic regions. Congress has mandated that "The Postal Service shall have as its basic function the obligation to provide postal services to bind the Nation together through the personal, educational, literary, and business correspondence of the people. It shall provide prompt, reliable, and efficient services to patrons in all areas and shall render postal services to all communities. The Postal Service shall provide a maximum degree of effective and regular postal services to rural areas, communities, and small towns where post offices are not self-sustaining."[11]

When it proposes rate increases (subject to Postal Rate Commission review), the Postal Service is required to consider the fairness, equity, and simplicity of its rate structure (across multiple services) as well as the relationships among prices, production costs, and the value of the service provided. Such mandates indicate that, in contrast to the typical private firm in a capitalist society, SOEs seldom seek solely to maximize the profit they generate. The profit SOEs are permitted to earn is often explicitly limited, and SOEs are commonly instructed to pursue goals that are distinct from, if not fundamentally incompatible with, profit maximization.[12]

In practice, an SOE is not a monolithic entity that faithfully executes its mandate. Rather, it is an organization comprised of many individuals, including managers who often have considerable discretion to pursue their own objectives. That discretion arises in part because SOEs are not subject to takeover threats and are generally less subject to the discipline of capital markets than private enterprises. Even though the managers of private, profit-maximizing firms may have goals and interests similar to those of managers in SOEs, the discipline of capital markets will limit the freedom of private managers to pursue private interests that do not maximize shareholder value.[13] Managers of SOEs (and government officials who monitor them) often have considerable interest in expanding the scale or scope of their activities, in part because a manager's abilities may be inferred from the size of the operations he or she oversees.[14]

This preference for expanded scale and scope of operations suggests that SOEs will act as if they maximize some combination of profit and operating scale. In practice, revenue often serves as a convenient proxy for scale.

In the formal analysis that underlies the discussion in this chapter, we rely on the simplifying assumption that SOEs value both revenue and profit. However, it is important to note that the key qualitative conclusions drawn from our analysis hold more generally. The conclusions hold, for example, if the SOE seeks to maximize a combination of output and profit or if it seeks to maximize revenue (or output) subject to the constraint that its profit exceed some specified level. The key assumption is that the SOE values revenue or output as well as profit. Its concern with revenue or output effectively induces the SOE to discount the cost of expanding output. Consequently, even though the SOE values the profit its anticompetitive activities can generate less highly than does a private profit-maximizing firm, the SOE pursues particularly aggressively anticompetitive activities that serve to expand its own output and revenue. In essence, the SOE's increased concern with output outweighs its reduced concern with profit in determining its interactions with competitors.

An SOE's Pricing

In the appendix to this chapter, we present a formal analysis of how SOEs set prices for their services when they seek to maximize a combination of profit and output. Here, we summarize the main findings from that analysis.[15] We find that a multiproduct SOE that maximizes a combination of profit and revenue effectively discounts the marginal costs of producing its services more than a private, profit-maximizing firm does. That is, when it determines prices for its goods and services, the SOE will be less concerned than its private counterpart about the extra cost it incurs when it expands its output. The greater its focus on revenue rather than profit, the more the SOE discounts marginal costs in pricing its goods and services.

This discounting of marginal costs reflects the fact that as the SOE becomes more concerned with revenue relative to profit, it becomes less averse to the higher costs that arise from increased output. Consequently, the SOE favors more highly the expanded output and revenue that result from low prices on those products for which competition from alternative suppliers is most pronounced. When such competition exists, a reduced focus on profit leads the SOE to set particularly low prices for the products on which it faces the most intense competition. Indeed, as John Lott has suggested, an SOE is likely to set the price of a product below its marginal cost of production, even in the absence of predatory intent.[16] We find that the SOE is particularly likely to prefer below-cost prices when its focus on profit is more limited and when customer demand for its products is more sensitive to price.[17]

This conclusion holds because even though profit declines as the SOE reduces price below marginal cost, revenue can increase as price declines. Therefore, if the SOE's relative valuation of revenue is sufficiently pronounced or if customer demand for some of its products is sufficiently sensitive to price (or both), then the SOE will choose to set some prices below marginal production costs. In doing so, the SOE may drive a more efficient competitor from the market.

Avoiding Restrictions on Below-Cost Pricing

The foregoing analysis considers the prices preferred by an SOE when its pricing flexibility is unrestricted. In practice, an SOE may face restrictions on its prices. For example, it might be prohibited from pricing below marginal cost, just as private, profit-maximizing firms typically are. We now explain how firms can relax a binding prohibition against below-cost pricing and why a public enterprise may have stronger incentives than a profit-maximizing firm to relax such a prohibition.

One obvious way in which a firm can relax a binding constraint against pricing below marginal cost is to manipulate accounting data to understate its actual marginal cost. Such understatement might be achieved by classifying as overhead production costs some or all of the costs that truly vary as output varies. For example, the firm might count some of the personnel hired to supply the product in question as central management. An alternate way for the firm to understate its true marginal cost is to record as variable costs incurred in the provision of a different product costs that are truly incurred in producing the product whose price the firm would like to set below marginal cost. For example, the firm might claim that materials and supplies employed to produce the product in question were employed to produce a different product.

Intentional understatement of marginal production costs entails personal risk. Laws against fraud carry severe financial penalties, and career prospects can be dimmed for managers who are suspected of knowingly reporting false information. But even if the SOE bears the full costs of the manipulation, the associated benefits may outweigh the costs. Most important, when the SOE values more highly than a private, profit-maximizing firm the expanded output and revenue that result from the lower price the understatement facilitates, the SOE will be more likely than its private counterpart to understate its costs. We therefore conclude that an SOE has a particularly strong incentive to understate its marginal cost of production to relax a binding prohibition against pricing below cost. The less profit-oriented the SOE, the greater this incentive will be.

Now consider a more subtle strategy an SOE might pursue to relax a binding prohibition against pricing below cost. Suppose that instead of misstating its true marginal cost, the SOE chooses to operate with an inefficient technology that secures a relatively low marginal cost at the expense of a particularly high overhead cost. In practice, a firm can do so by installing general-purpose equipment on a large scale, thereby reducing the need for project-specific equipment. It can also do so by, for example, retaining a large on-site staff with broad legal, engineering, computing, and/or marketing expertise that substitutes for specific expertise on individual products.

More generally, suppose the SOE has a choice among production technologies and suppose this choice is measured by the amount of an overhead resource the firm employs. For expositional convenience, we refer to this resource as *capital*.[18] The more capital the firm installs, the lower its variable and marginal costs of production will be. Therefore, because an SOE values highly the expanded scale and scope facilitated by low marginal production costs, it has particularly strong incentives to overinvest in capital to relax a binding prohibition on pricing below cost.[19]

The more highly the SOE values expanded scale and scope relative to profit, the more it benefits from the expanded scale a lower price provides and the less concerned it is with the associated cost. Therefore, the less concerned the SOE is with generating profit, the greater the technological inefficiency it will endure to secure a lower price and the expanded scale it engenders. Such inefficient overcapitalization can be particularly pronounced if the SOE's capital purchases are subsidized (as they can be, for example if the SOE is afforded privileged access to government funds).

For simplicity, our discussion focuses on the case in which the cost of producing each product is independent of the cost of producing other products. However, the presence of cost complementarities (where the production of one good lowers the cost of producing another) can provide an SOE with an additional means to relax a binding prohibition on pricing below cost. To illustrate, suppose the SOE produces two products, A and B. Further suppose the SOE is, by law, the sole supplier of product A, whereas both the SOE and competitors supply product B. Finally, suppose there are economies of scope in the provision of products A and B that cause the SOE's marginal cost of producing B to decline as its supply of product A increases. In the presence of such cost complementarities, the SOE can enjoy a lower marginal cost for product B by increasing its output of product A. This output expansion might be accomplished, for example, by agreeing to take on an expanded universal service obligation in the delivery of product A.

Consequently, when cost complementarities are present, an SOE gains in two distinct ways from accepting an expanded universal service obligation. First, it increases the scale and scope of the SOE's monopoly operations. Second, it reduces the SOE's cost of supplying product B. This reduction in marginal cost typically serves to expand the SOE's production of product B. It is of particular value in this regard when the SOE faces a binding restriction on pricing below cost.

In sum, an SOE's preference for expanded scale and scope can leave it with strong incentives to disadvantage competitors by strategically relaxing a binding prohibition against below-cost pricing in a variety of ways.

Raising Rivals' Costs

To disadvantage their rivals, firms can undertake activities other than strategically relaxing a binding prohibition against below-cost pricing. For example, firms might lobby for regulations that increase rivals' operating costs, restrict rivals' access to essential productive inputs, and buy excessive amounts of inputs to raise the market price of those inputs.[20]

A public enterprise has particularly strong incentives to raise the costs of its competitors by undertaking such activities. When it raises its rivals' costs, the SOE induces its profit-maximizing competitors to reduce the amount of output they choose to sell to customers and/or to increase the prices they charge for their products. Those actions by competitors serve to increase customer demand for the SOE's products, which promotes an expanded scale of operation for the SOE.

Private profit-maximizing competitors enjoy the extra profit they secure when their rivals are disadvantaged. If public enterprises value profit less highly than private firms, it is conceivable that they might be less inclined to disadvantage their rivals. Often, however, the opposite is true. A reduced focus on profit can cause an SOE to be more aggressive in raising its rivals' costs and render the cost of expanded output less onerous for a public enterprise. Because an SOE will pursue the expanded scale it values highly by reducing the output of its rivals by raising their costs, we can conclude that an SOE may have stronger incentives than a private, profit-maximizing firm to raise its rivals' costs. Furthermore, the less profit-oriented the enterprise, the more pronounced such incentives will be for the SOE.[21]

In addition to raising the operating costs of an existing rival, an SOE might undertake activities designed to preclude the operation of potential rivals. For example, it might lobby key policymakers to erect impenetrable entry barriers, such as statutory prohibitions on entry. When successful competitors reduce an SOE's ability to expand the scale and scope of its operations, the SOE has strong incentives to limit the success of those competitors. Often, the more highly the SOE values expanded scale relative to profit, the more pronounced this preference becomes. We thus find that an SOE has strong incentives to undertake activities designed to exclude competitors from the marketplace whenever successful competition would reduce its output. These incentives increase as the SOE becomes less profit oriented.

Economies of Scope between Monopolized and Competitive Markets

The pronounced desire of the SOE to exclude rivals arises even in the absence of cost complementarities. For the reasons identified above, this desire will become more pronounced when cost complementarities are present. In particular, when the exclusion of rivals in one market serves to increase the SOE's output in that market, its operating costs decline in a second market. That cost reduction, in turn, expands the SOE's scale of operation in the second market.

If the SOE operates in both a monopolized market (such as letter delivery services) served only by the SOE and a competitive market (such as parcel delivery services) served by the SOE and one or more rivals, then the SOE can exploit economies of scope (cost complementarities) between the two markets. A statutory monopoly, however, truncates the range of services an entrant can offer in competition with an SOE. The effect of the monopolized area is to prevent an efficient entrant from achieving economies of scope and thus lowering its marginal cost of supplying the competitive product. Although similar to the raising-rivals'-costs strategy described above, this strategy is more accurately described as denying rivals the opportunity to lower their costs.[22] All other things remaining constant, the rival faces higher costs in the competitive market than the SOE experiences. We call this the direct effect of the statutory monopoly in the competitive market.

In addition to this direct effect, an indirect effect arises if economies of scale exist in the competitive market. If the SOE sets a lower price in the competitive market because of the realized economies of scope, demand will shift from the rival to the SOE. As the SOE's output of the competitive product increases, the SOE experiences economies of scale its rivals cannot achieve. The resulting decline in the SOE's unit cost of operation in the competitive market causes a further shift in sales from competitors to the SOE depending on the SOE's objectives and the nature of the competitive interaction between the SOE and its rivals.

The key conclusion here is that the SOE derives from its statutory monopoly over the monopolized product an incremental benefit in the form of both economies of scope and economies of scale in the competitive market. These combined effects, direct and indirect, are not the intended consequence of the government granting the SOE a statutory monopoly in the monopolized market. Both incremental effects flow causally from the statutory monopoly and not from an inherent cost advantage that only the SOE enjoys.

In sum, the diverse goals of a public enterprise lead it to act more aggressively toward its rivals than does a private enterprise. A reduced focus on profit leads the SOE to price competitive products below cost. It can also increase the SOE's incentive to raise the costs of existing rivals, to erect entry barriers to preclude entry by potential rivals, and to understate costs and adopt inefficient production technologies to circumvent regulations designed to foster competition. Each of these activities precludes the operation of more efficient competitors and thereby reduces social welfare. So, too, can the advantages an SOE enjoys in competitive markets when it, alone, is authorized to operate in monopolized markets.

These findings influence the optimal design of competition law as applied to public enterprises. Because an SOE has greater incentive to engage in anticompetitive practices and circumvent antitrust laws than its private counterpart, particular vigilance in monitoring the market activities of SOEs is warranted. It may also be appropriate to subject an SOE to more stringent competition laws and harsher penalties for violating them.

The Ability of State-Owned Enterprises to Act Anticompetitively

Until recently, an unstated premise in the intellectual literature on pricing had been that the alleged predator is a privately owned firm that seeks to maximize profit. A profit-maximizing firm will undertake predatory pricing only if doing so is expected to increase long-term profit. But a public enterprise typically does not seek to maximize long-term profit. Thus, for the reasons explained above, an SOE has greater incentive than a private firm to charge below-cost prices. In addition, an SOE typically has enhanced ability to charge below-cost prices and otherwise disadvantage competitors for at least five reasons.

First, the legislation that creates an SOE usually imposes upon it the duty, or confers upon it the prerogative, to pursue objectives other than profit maximization—such as provision of universal service at a uniform, geographically averaged price. This duty or prerogative endows an SOE with greater ability than a private, profit-maximizing firm to sustain prices below costs for extended periods of time. In its October 1999 report on competition in postal services, the Committee on Competition Law and Policy of the Organization for Economic Cooperation and Development (OECD) observed, "In practice the vast majority of incumbent postal operators are state-owned. The precise objectives of state-owned firms are contested, and probably differ according to the governance arrangements for state-owned firms in each country, but generally-speaking profit-maximisation is typically merely one amongst a number of objectives pursued by such firms. Where a firm, for whatever reason, does not seek to strictly maximise profits, it may be able to sustain prices below cost indefinitely, supported by either prices above cost in some other segment or by some other source of funds."[23] The very decision to create an SOE suggests that the firm embodies an attempt by government to rectify a perceived market failure or to advance a desired social objective, such as income redistribution, through means other than profit maximization.

Second, an SOE need not recoup losses by ultimately raising prices in the competitive market. This feature of public ownership is in direct contrast to the scholarship and jurisprudence on predatory pricing by private firms, which emphasize that after the exit of competitors or the prevention of entry, the dominant firm will seek to raise the price sufficiently above the competitive level long enough to recoup the earlier profit sacrifice and more.[24] Unlike a private utility subject to rate-of-return or price-cap regulation, an SOE has substantial ability to carry losses forward into future periods of the ratemaking process.[25]

More important, unlike a private firm, an SOE has substantial ability to recoup its losses by raising prices in monopolized markets where it has a statutory monopoly or via direct expenditures from the public treasury. The EC, for example, found that the letter-mail monopoly in Germany produced "a guaranteed source of income exceeding stand-alone cost" during the period covered by the *Deutsche Post* case.[26] The OECD noted that, in the case of a public enterprise, predatory pricing is a subset of distortionary pricing, which does not necessarily require conventional recoupment of losses: "It is convenient . . . to label pricing below cost as "distortionary." "Predatory" pricing is a temporary form of distortionary pricing. Even where distortionary pricing does not lead to prices subsequently being raised above cost, it may still be of public policy concern, because of the effect on productive efficiency. Distortionary pricing might induce a more efficient firm to leave or to not enter the competitive market."[27]

Third, unlike the private firm, which may find it impossible to repel entry when prices ultimately rise to profitable levels, SOEs may be able to preclude such entry. This ability arises because SOEs are often multiproduct firms that benefit from statutory monopolies over related products or services. The U.S. Postal Service, for example, has the discretion to interpret the contours of its own statutory monopoly.[28] Thus, the Postal Service enjoys the ability to raise entry costs for private firms by defining the scope of competitive services that can be supplied privately.

Fourth, an SOE enjoys privileges and immunities (apart from explicit state subsidies of operating losses) that facilitate recoupment of losses incurred in noncore markets or that make them irrelevant. The U.S. Postal Service, for example, has no obligation to compensate its investors, the American taxpayers. The absence of an obligation to pay a competitive return on invested capital lowers the cost of funds an SOE can use to subsidize losses in noncore markets. In addition, an SOE may be exempt from taxation, which reduces its operating costs.[29]

Fifth, an SOE may be subject to less binding price regulation than is the typical private firm subject to regulation. The less binding nature of the price regulation can arise, for example, because the regulatory agency overseeing the SOE's operation has a limited set of policy instruments at its disposal. For example, the U.S. Postal Rate Commission lacks subpoena power, and its powers to set maximum prices for postal services are not unlimited. Thus, in general, an SOE has a heightened opportunity to engage in anticompetitive behavior, including below-cost pricing.[30]

These are only five of the many reasons SOEs may have greater ability than their private, profit-maximizing counterparts to engage in anticompetitive activities. Policymakers increasingly are recognizing that this greater ability, coupled with a corresponding greater incentive of SOEs to disadvantage rivals, deserves the heightened scrutiny of competition authorities.[31]

Conclusion

In American jurisprudence, competition law for state-owned enterprises is limited. However, the EC's decision in the *Deutsche Post* case in 2001 establishes an important precedent that could soon affect the United States if the arbitration panel in the *Canada Post* case filed under Chapter 11 of NAFTA is influenced by the EC's decision. The challenge ahead is to infuse emerging legal principles in such cases with sound economic analysis that reflects the special characteristics of public enterprises and the network industries in which SOEs commonly operate.

We have explained why SOEs have strong incentives to engage in anticompetitive activities that serve to expand the scale and scope of their operations. When an SOE values both profit and expanded scale, it discounts the cost of output expansion. Consequently, even though such an SOE values the profit its anticompetitive activities generate less highly than does a private profit-maximizing firm, the SOE pursues aggressively anticompetitive activities that expand the scale of its operations. In particular, an SOE will set prices below marginal production costs, especially on products for which demand is sensitive to price. An SOE also may understate its marginal cost of production and overinvest in capacity to relax a binding prohibition on pricing below cost. In addition, an SOE has stronger incentives than a private, profit-maximizing firm to raise its rivals' costs and to undertake activities designed to exclude rivals from relevant markets.

SOEs also commonly have enhanced ability to engage in anticompetitive activities relative to private firms. This enhanced ability stems from several sources. For example, SOEs often enjoy privileges and immunities that afford them considerable discretion in the activities they undertake. In addition, an SOE's legal framework may impose upon it the duty, or confer upon it the prerogative, to pursue objectives other than profit maximization. Furthermore, SOEs often are multiproduct firms that benefit from statutory monopolies over related products. Consequently, SOEs, unlike their private competitors, may not need to recoup the costs of anticompetitive activities by raising prices in competitive markets.

In light of the greater incentive and ability of SOEs to engage in anticompetitive activities, enhanced scrutiny of SOEs under antitrust law is appropriate. Furthermore, because a monopoly position in one market enables an SOE to reduce competition in another market, it is wise to construe narrowly any statutory monopoly that is conferred upon it. In addition, strict limits on an SOE's ability to expand beyond the market covered by its statutory monopoly may be appropriate.

Appendix: A Formal Analysis of SOE Pricing

We explained in the text why an SOE has the incentive to maximize a combination of revenues and profits. Here we develop formally the pricing decisions implied by that behavior.

Different SOEs may value revenues and profits differently. To capture differences among SOEs, we employ the parameter w, which can range from 0 to 1, to denote the weight an SOE places on revenue. We let $1 - w$ denote the corresponding weight on profit. By varying w, we can capture the objectives of different SOEs.

The following additional notation permits a formal statement of the class of objective functions under consideration. Let $n \geq 1$ denote the number of products supplied by the SOE. Also let $p_i \geq 0$ denote the price the SOE charges for its i-th product, and let $p \equiv (p_1, \ldots, p_n)$ denote the prices the SOE charges for its n products. In addition, let $Q_i(p)$ denote the amount of product i that customers will buy when the SOE sets prices p (customers will buy more of any product the lower is its price). $Q \equiv (Q_1(p), \ldots, Q_n(p))$ will denote all of the output produced by the SOE. For simplicity, the ensuing analysis focuses on the setting in which customer demand for each of the SOE's products is independent of the prices charged for other products. The function $C(Q)$ denotes the SOE's cost of producing output Q.[32]

This notation enables us to specify the SOE's objective, which is to maximize

$$w \left[\sum_{i=1}^{n} p_i Q_i(p) \right] + [1-w] \left[\sum_{i=1}^{n} p_i Q_i(p) - C(Q) \right]. \qquad (1)$$

The first term in square brackets in expression (1) is the SOE's total revenue. Total revenue is the sum of the revenue derived from the sale of each of the SOE's n products. The revenue derived from the sale of any particular product (i) is simply the product of the number of units of the product sold (Q_i) and the price (p_i) at which each unit is sold. The last term in square brackets in expression (1) is the SOE's profit. Profit is the difference between total revenue and total operating cost. Thus, with the weight w applied to revenue and the weight $[1 - w]$ applied to profit, expression (1) is simply the aforementioned weighted average of revenue and profit.

Before discussing the prices preferred by an SOE that maximizes a weighted average of revenue and profit, we consider the prices that a private, profit-maximizing firm would set in the simple, static setting described above. It is well known that a firm will maximize profit in this setting by raising prices above marginal production costs by amounts that are inversely proportional to the sensitivity of customer demand to price.[33] In other words, the firm will set the price for a product close to its marginal cost of production when a higher price would cause many potential customers to decide not to purchase the product. In contrast, on products for which customer purchases do not decline much in response to price increases, the profit-maximizing firm will set prices well above marginal production costs.

This pricing strategy is summarized formally in Finding 1. The Finding refers to $\epsilon_i = |[\partial Q_i / \partial p_i][p_i / Q_i]|$, which is the own-price elasticity of demand for product i. The price elasticity of demand for product i measures the rate at which customer purchases decline as the price of product i increases. The larger the price elasticity of demand for a product, the more pronounced the decline in customer purchases as the price of the product increases.

Finding 1. The preferred prices of a profit-maximizing multiproduct firm are characterized by the following inverse-elasticity rule:

$$\frac{p_i - \dfrac{\partial C(Q)}{\partial Q_i}}{p_i} = \frac{1}{\varepsilon_i}, \qquad \text{for } i = 1, \ldots, n. \tag{2}$$

Expression (2) indicates that the profit-maximizing firm will always set the price of each of its products above its marginal cost of production.[34] In the simple, static setting considered here, reducing a price below marginal cost serves only to reduce profit, and so such pricing is not attractive to the profit-maximizing firm.

Now consider the prices preferred by a multiproduct SOE that seeks to maximize a weighted average of revenue and profit in the same setting. The prices that maximize expression (1) are characterized in Finding 2.

Finding 2. **The SOE's preferred prices are characterized by the following modified inverse-elasticity rule:**

$$\frac{p_i - [1-w]\dfrac{\partial C(Q)}{\partial Q_i}}{p_i} = \frac{1}{\varepsilon_i}, \qquad \text{for } i = 1, \ldots, n. \qquad (3)$$

Finding 2 reveals that the prices preferred by an SOE that seeks to maximize expression (1) follow a modified inverse-elasticity rule. To maximize a weighted average of revenue and profit, the SOE implements proportional markups of price over modified marginal cost, $[1 - w]\partial C(Q)/\partial Q_i$, that vary inversely with the price elasticity of demand. The more inelastic the demand for the product, the further above modified marginal cost the prices are set.

Expressions (2) and (3) reveal that the SOE's pricing rule is the same rule that a profit-maximizing firm follows, except that marginal costs are scaled down by the factor $[1 - w]$ to reflect the SOE's reduced focus on profit. The greater its focus on revenue rather than profit (that is, the larger is w), the more the SOE discounts marginal costs in the modified inverse-elasticity rule. It is apparent from expression (3) that even in the absence of predatory intent, an SOE may set the prices for some of its products below their marginal costs of production. The SOE will be particularly likely to prefer below-cost prices when its focus on profit is more limited and when customer demand for its products is more sensitive to price.

Notes

1. World Bank, *Bureaucrats in Business: The Economics and Politics of Government Ownership* (Oxford: Oxford University Press, 1995), 30.
2. We use the term *anticompetitive* instead of *predatory* because the latter often connotes that the firm recoups losses from below-cost pricing after it causes rivals to exit the market or desist from aggressive competition. An SOE may not need to recoup such losses, for reasons we explain.
3. Because European nations, among others, typically do not employ the term *antitrust law*, it would be parochial to use that term to describe the developing body of law on SOEs. Instead, we employ the term *competition law*.
4. See, for example, John Vickers and George Yarrow, *Privatization: An Economic Analysis* (Cambridge: MIT Press, 1988).
5. See Edmund L. Andrews, "Merge? Yes and Non," in *New York Times*, 8 July 2001, sect. 4, 2.
6. Case COMP/35.141, Deutsche Post AG, 2001 O.J. (L 125) 27 at ¶ 36.
7. *Flamingo Indus. (USA) Ltd v. U.S. Postal Serv.*, 302 F.3d 985, 988–89 (9th Cir. 2002).
8. *Flamingo Industries*, 302 F.3d at 989 (quoting 39 U.S.C. § 401(1)).
9. *United Parcel Service of America, Inc. v. Canada: Notice of Intent to Submit a Claim to Arbitration Under Section B of Chapter 11 of the North American Free Trade Agreement* 1, 12 (19 Jan. 2000), available at http://www.dfait-maeci.gc.ca/tna-nac/ups-noi.pdf.
10. The marginal cost of product X refers to the increase in the firm's total outlays that result from a small increase in the output of X.
11. 39 U.S.C. § 101.
12. If an SOE is not maximizing its profits, it necessarily is not minimizing its losses. Operating losses are the difference between total cost and total revenue. To say that an SOE seeks to price to minimize its losses in a competitive market is to say that it chooses a price that minimizes the difference between total cost and total revenue. This is the same price that maximizes the difference between total revenue and total costs.

13. See R. Richard Geddes, "Agency Costs and Governance in the United States Postal Service," in J. Gregory Sidak, *Governing the Postal Service* (Washington, D.C.: AEI Press, 1994).

14. In summarizing the relevant empirical evidence, Andre Blais and Stephane Dion conclude that bureaucrats may seek to expand the scale of their operations (by securing larger budgets) to realize the power and prestige that often accompany expanded operations. Expanded output can also promote expanded employment, which can be a goal of SOEs. See Andre Blais and Stephane Dion, "Conclusion: Are Bureaucrats Budget Maximizers?," in Andre Blais and Stephane Dion, *The Budget-Maximizing Bureaucrat: Appraisals and Evidence* (Pittsburgh: Pittsburgh University Press, 1991), 355.

15. For further discussion and analysis, see David E. M. Sappington and J. G. Sidak, "Incentives for Anticompetitive Behavior by Public Enterprises," in *The Review of Industrial Organization* 22 (2003): 183–206.

16. John R. Lott Jr., "Predation by Public Enterprises," *Journal of Public Economics* 43 (1990): 237.

17. See the appendix to this chapter for a formal demonstration of this point.

18. The overhead cost could include labor. The critical feature of overhead cost is that it does not vary with the level of output produced by the firm.

19. For a related insight in the context of a regulated firm, see Kenneth Baseman, "Open Entry and Cross-Subsidization in Regulated Markets," in Gary Fromm, *Studies in Public Regulation* (Cambridge: MIT Press, 1981).

20. See Steven Salop and David Scheffman, "Raising Rivals' Costs," *American Economic Review* 73 (1983): 267–71; Steven Salop and David Scheffman, "Cost-Raising Strategies," *Journal of Industrial Economics* 36 (1987): 19–34.

21. Notice that when cost complementarities are present, rivals' costs can be increased simply by the fact that they are precluded from operating in markets that are reserved exclusively for an SOE. As we explain in greater detail, the mere presence of a monopolized market can prevent rivals from reducing their costs to the level enjoyed by an SOE, even in the absence of any deliberate attempt by the SOE to raise its rivals' costs.

22. In the *Deutsche Post* case, for example, the EC noted that "joint deliv-

eries [of mail-order parcels and letters] create economies of scope that exist between the monopolized product and the competitive product. Due to the monopolized area these economies of scope are not available to competitors." Case COMP/35.141, Deutsche Post AG, 2001 O.J. (L 125) 27 at ¶ 11 n.17.

23. Organization for Economic Cooperation and Development, Committee on Competition Law and Policy, *Promoting Competition in Postal Service* (No. 24, DAFEE/CLP (99)22, 1 October 1999), 55.

24. See Philip Areeda and Donald F. Turner, "Predatory Pricing and Related Practices Under Section 2 of the Sherman Act," *Harvard Law Review* 88 (1975): 697–733; William J. Baumol, "Predation and the Logic of the Average Variable Cost Test," *Journal of Law Economics* 39 (1996): 49–72.

25. For an application to the U.S. Postal Service, see J. Gregory Sidak and Daniel F. Spulber, *Protecting Competition from the Postal Monopoly* (Washington, D.C.: AEI Press, 1996), 116.

26. Case COMP/35.141, Deutsche Post AG, 2001 O.J. (L 125) 27, p.32, n. 52. The stand-alone cost of service X is the outlay that would be required for a firm to produce service X and no other service.

27. Organization for Economic Cooperation and Development, Committee on Competition Law and Policy, *Promoting Competition in Postal Service* (No. 24, DAFEE/CLP (99)22, 1 October 1999): 55.

28. See Sidak and Spulber, *Protecting Competition from the Postal Monopoly*, 18–19, 26–31.

29. The U.S. Postal Service is exempt from taxation. See Sidak and Spulber, *Protecting Competition from the Postal Monopoly*, 2.

30. In the United States, for example, there is a significant risk of anticompetitive cost misallocation by the U.S. Postal Service despite the fact that its independent regulator, the Postal Rate Commission, regularly presides over adversarial, evidentiary rate cases that often last nine months or more. See Sidak and Spulber, *Protecting Competition from the Postal Monopoly*, 101–46.

31. See, for example, Organization for Economic Cooperation and Development, Committee on Competition Law and Policy, *Promoting Competition in Postal Service* (No. 24, DAFEE/CLP (99) 22, 1 October 1999), 55, 336–37 (Aide Memoire of the Discussion).

32. In this simple setting with independent demands, $\partial Q_i(p)/\partial p_j = 0$ for

all $j \neq i$, and so the demand for the SOE's i-th product can be written as $Q_i(\mathbf{p}_i)$.

33. See Frank Ramsey, "A Contribution to the Theory of Taxation," *Economic Journal* 37 (1927): 47–61; William J. Baumol and David F. Bradford, "Optimal Departures From Marginal Cost Pricing," *American Economic Review* 60 (1970): 265–83.

34. This conclusion follows because the price elasticity of demand is always a positive number. Therefore, the term to the right of the equal sign in expression (2) is positive, which implies that the expression to the left of the equal sign must also be positive. This latter expression will be positive only if price (p_i) exceeds marginal cost ($\partial C(Q)/\partial Q_i$).

Chapter 2

Case Studies of Anticompetitive SOE Behavior

R. Richard Geddes

Direct competition between state-owned enterprises (SOEs) or government-sponsored enterprises (GSEs) and privately owned, unsubsidized firms occurs more frequently than is commonly appreciated. It is, or historically has occurred, in the provision of electricity, water, financial services, postal services, weather forecasting, information, freight transport, mortgage lending, and many other activities. Where possible, GSEs and SOEs will expand their revenue base by venturing into new, competitive business lines. They will underprice in those businesses in which they compete directly with private firms and will engage in a variety of other anticompetitive activities. These activities are discussed by David Sappington and Gregory Sidak in Chapter 1.

Scholars have rarely focused on such behavior. That is surprising because academic economists accept that private, regulated firms are inclined to shift costs onto their core, monopolized activities and away from activities in which they face competition. For example, it has been shown that regulated, investor-owned utilities that have other commercial business interests will shift overhead costs onto the regulated activity.[1] Defense contractors with both sole-source contracts and commercial products facing competition will shift costs to their sole-source contracts, where they face less competition.[2] Hospitals are inclined to shift costs from payers using fixed-price reimbursement methods to those using reported costs.[3]

As Sappington and Sidak suggest, SOEs and GSEs are likely to engage in similar cost-shifting behavior when they face competition from private firms. In this chapter, I catalog a number of cases of such competition. I first review the government-granted advantages that SOEs and GSEs typically enjoy and then examine ways in which those privileges allow them to successfully compete with private firms even though they may be less efficient. I discuss cases in which government and private unsubsidized firms compete and consider the lessons and implications of those cases.

This chapter is not intended to provide an exhaustive list of all instances of government-private competition or to provide a definitive treatment of each case. Rather, it is to demonstrate that such competition is a general phenomenon and that similar issues arise in each case. Collectively, the case studies presented here suggest that concerns about cost shifting in other industries are also appropriate when government and private firms compete.

Special Privileges and Immunities Enjoyed by SOEs and GSEs

SOEs and GSEs enjoy a variety of government-granted subsidies, privileges, and immunities. Those privileges give government firms an artificial competitive advantage over private rivals.[4] By artificial I mean that the firm's competitive advantage is not based on superior management skills, more efficient technology, enhanced innovation, better negotiating techniques, or indeed on any other economic factor. Its competitive advantage is government created.

Inefficient competition between government and private firms occurs when SOEs and GSEs use government-granted privileges and immunities to price below private rivals that would be lower cost in the absence of those benefits. That is, special privileges and immunities distort the prices offered by SOEs and GSEs. Such behavior has several harmful effects. First, there is a direct misallocation of resources because prices do not reflect true economic cost. The true economic cost of an enterprise includes, for example, tax payments, undistorted interest payments on debt, a market return on equity, and the cost of complying with reporting requirements, among many others. Prices in competitive markets should reflect those costs. Second, as Sappington and Sidak showed in Chapter 1, a government firm will be willing to set price even below the subsidized cost it actually faces and keep it there without regard to long-term losses.

Third, more efficient but unsubsidized private firms will contract, not invest, or may not start up if they observe or anticipate competition from a government rival. If there is uncertainty over the government firm's intention or ability to expand into a particular activity, that uncertainty will contribute to private disinvestment.

Fourth, if a government firm prices below cost, then less (or none) of its overhead costs will be covered by the price of the service, which means that taxpayers (or some other captive group) must pay for more of the cost of the overhead. Such competition is thus also a drain on the taxpayer.

Although specific institutional arrangements vary across particular organizations, the privileges discussed below are common. Each can be used to artificially expand SOE or GSE revenues where it faces competition.

Monopoly Power

Government firms often receive explicit government-protected monopolies in their core activities. For example, the federal government

grants the U.S. Postal Service exclusive monopolies over both the
delivery of letter mail and over the use of customers' mailboxes. Amtrak has a monopoly over the carriage of passengers on intercity railroad routes. Electric utilities (federal, state, municipal, and private)
often possess geographic monopolies over their service territories.

The implication of monopoly power for anticompetitive behavior is straightforward. A government firm can shift costs onto activities in which customers are held captive to the monopoly and away
from activities where it faces competition. Stated differently, it can
use economic profits (or rents) from its monopolized activities to
cross subsidize (or underprice) in activities where it faces competition.

Legally enforced monopoly creates significant, legitimate anticompetitive concerns. However, there are at least six additional gov-
ernment-bestowed privileges and immunities typically granted to
SOEs and GSEs. Because money is fungible, the government firm
can shift rents from each to help sustain inefficient competition with
private rivals.

Credit Guarantees

Government firms can borrow at taxpayer-guaranteed preferential
rates, which artificially reduces borrowing costs. The guarantee is
either explicit or implicit. The Postal Service, for example, is allowed
to borrow directly from the Federal Financing Bank. The federal government guarantees its debt. The TVA also enjoys a government debt
guarantee. As a result, both firms have saved enormous amounts on
debt service due to lower interest payments. As Paul MacAvoy and
George McIssac state, "The public enterprises have had special access to capital through the Federal Financial Bank (FFB) which guarantees public bonds at interest charges less than market rates for
private companies of comparable risk. Both TVA and USPS financed
their placements of debt with the FFB at a 12.5 basis-point premium

above Treasury bond rates. This rate was lower than on bonds of companies with comparable financial performance. . . . If these organizations had not had access to FFB financing, the additional interest charges which they would have incurred would have exceeded $5 billion over the first half of the 1980s."[5]

Even if firms do not possess explicit government-provided credit guarantees, financial markets view those firms as possessing implicit guarantees if the government would disallow default. Fannie Mae and Freddie Mac are viewed as possessing an implicit government debt guarantee. The savings from lower interest rates as a result of an implicit guarantee are also substantial. By lowering debt costs, express or implied government debt guarantees artificially enhance an SOE's or a GSE's ability to price below rivals offering competitive services.

Captive Equity

By captive equity I refer to the fact that in an SOE, equity is locked in the firm, whereas in a private, publicly traded corporation, equity shares are transferable. Taxpayer-owners, who funded the government firm's original capital stock, are prohibited from withdrawing their funds in the event of poor firm performance. The use of legal coercion to keep capital within the firm is a (perhaps *the*) unique feature of government ownership.

Captive equity is a frequently overlooked subsidy to SOEs, but it is important for several reasons. First, because of captive equity, government-owned firms are absolved from paying dividends or indeed any expected return to shareholders to induce them to contribute capital to the firm. That, in addition to any express or implied debt guarantee, artificially lowers the cost of capital relative to that of a privately owned, publicly traded corporation. Conversely, government firms are free to dissipate owners' equity through consistent losses over time without fear of the owners selling their equity stake.

Government firms can use that lower cost of capital to subsidize activities in which they face competition.

Second, captive equity removes a key market-based constraint on pricing products and services below cost. When private firms price below cost in an attempt to drive out a rival firm, it is known as predatory pricing. Predatory pricing by private firms is rarely profitable.[6] A predatory firm must not only price below cost but also expand output at that low price and maintain its low price long enough to drive the rival out.

Because they create stock prices, tradable ownership shares constrain private corporations from predatory pricing. Stock prices fall rapidly when losses are incurred because of below-cost pricing. If the wealth of managers is tied to performance of the firm (through bonuses, restricted stock, or stock options) as is typical in most large corporations, then managers' wealth will decline if they predate. Managers of private firms thus have little incentive to predatory price.

Managers of government-owned firms, however, face no such constraint. There are, by definition, no stock prices to react to the firm's below-cost pricing. SOE managers' wealth will not be reduced by predation. Instead, the manager is likely to value the increased output associated with predation for its own sake and can indulge that preference with impunity. If the firm is not profit maximizing, there is no need to subsequently raise prices to recoup losses from predation. In addition to directly lowering the cost of equity, captive equity removes any market-based constraint on below-cost pricing.

Exemption from Bankruptcy

The companion privilege to captive equity is exemption from bankruptcy. Because owners cannot withdraw capital, government firms can operate for years while earning losses long after private firms would have gone bankrupt. Amtrak, for example, lost $908 million in 2000, $819 million in 2001, and $752 million in 2002. The U.S. Postal Service lost $200 million in 2000, $1.7 billion in 2001, and $676 million in 2002. Both firms continue to operate, which indicates that they can sustain long-term losses in activities where they face competition.

The lack of a bankruptcy constraint confers an artificial competitive advantage on government firms. As Michael Crew and Paul Kleindorfer observed, "In addition, a public enterprise is not subject to the pressure of competition in the same way that a private company is, in that it is insulated from bankruptcy. The insulation from the discipline of bankruptcy also means that a public enterprise, unless strongly reined in by government, can get into competitive ventures on favorable terms and therefore compete unfairly and inefficiently with privately owned companies."[7]

In addition to actually reducing the revenues of a private rival through lack of a bankruptcy constraint, the perception that an SOE or a GSE does not face bankruptcy is likely to discourage a private competitor from entering into or investing in an activity in which it might face government competition.

As with captive equity, there are subbenefits from a bankruptcy exemption. Because Amtrak has never earned a profit, for example, it has successfully avoided paying corporate income tax, to which it is in principle subject.

Tax Exemptions

Government firms are often exempt from various taxes to which private firms are subject. For example, Fannie Mae, Freddie Mac, Amtrak, the Tennessee Valley Authority, and the Postal Service, among others, are exempt from paying certain taxes. Such an exemption is a selective subsidy. It artificially lowers the government firm's costs and thus enhances its ability to price below more efficient, but taxed, rivals offering competitive services. Tax exemption also lowers an SOE's cost of tax calculation and tax council.

Direct Subsidies

Some SOEs receive direct government subsidies to defray capital and operating costs. Amtrak, for example, has never made money in its entire 32-year history. As of 2002, it had received over $44 billion (in 2002 dollars) in direct federal subsidies since it began operations in 1971. Until 1983, the Postal Service received a general public service subsidy. Perhaps because they are such transparent assistance (and a drain on the Treasury), direct subsidies are somewhat rare compared to other government-granted privileges.

Regulatory Exemptions

Government firms are often immune from a variety of regulatory requirements to which private firms are subject. For example, the Postal Service, Amtrak, and the TVA are immune from antitrust prosecution.[8] Additionally, because they do not have tradable ownership shares, SOEs and GSEs are not subject to the same costly SEC disclosure requirements as privately owned, publicly traded corporations. Government firms may also be exempt from certain environmental and health and safety regulations.

Other Government-Granted Privileges

There are a variety of additional government-granted privileges and immunities that apply to government firms on a case-by-case basis. The Postal Service, for example, has the power of eminent domain. It is immune from paying parking tickets for its vehicles and from paying for vehicle registrations. It can also purchase fuel tax exempt. It does not have to apply for building permits or conform to local zoning regulations. Clearly, the institutional details of each firm should be examined carefully for a full accounting of all government-granted privileges and immunities.

Anticompetitive Uses of Government-Granted Privileges

The array of privileges, immunities, and subsidies potentially enjoyed by SOEs and GSEs allows them to set prices below those of more economically efficient private rivals and enhances their ability to unnaturally force those rivals out. There are several ways in which a government firm can use those advantages to inefficiently compete with rivals not enjoying government-granted advantages.

Perhaps the most straightforward way for a government firm to use the privileges enumerated above in an anticompetitive fashion is to shift costs away from competitive and onto monopolized activities. Even though a private rival may be more efficient, the government firm can, by pricing services below cost, reduce the rival's share of the market, force it out of business entirely, or deter its entry. That phenomenon is often termed *cross subsidization*, reflecting the prevailing view that the government firm uses rents from monopolized activities to subsidize competitive activities.

The term is misleading however. Because money is fungible, the government operator can use the entire array of benefits discussed above, in addition to monopoly rents, to inefficiently subsidize activities where it faces competition. To recap, in addition to monopoly power, those rent sources include credit guarantees, immunity from paying investors an expected rate of return, exemption from bankruptcy, tax exemptions, direct subsidies, and immunity from antitrust prosecution, disclosure requirements, and other regulations. All such privileges and immunities are valuable and, absent preventive policies, can be used at the government firm's discretion. If the government firm values output or size, per se, then it will use those rents to reduce prices, thus expanding output, in activities where it faces competition.

The mechanism used by a government firm to cross subsidize activities in which it faces private competition can be more complex than direct cross subsidy. There are various institutional arrangements that allow a government-subsidized firm to transfer subsidies to another, affiliated firm. For example, the government-subsidized firm may form a joint venture with another, previously unsubsidized firm. It can then transfer subsidies to its venture partner, allowing the partner to inefficiently compete with unsubsidized rivals.

Similar to joint ventures, mergers and acquisitions provide an opportunity for a government-subsidized firm to inefficiently subsidize activities in which it faces competition. The government firm can shift rents to its acquisition, which may operate in a competitive market.

Joint ventures and acquisitions between government and private, previously unsubsidized firms are common in the postal industry, for example. Post Denmark, Finland Post, Norway Post, and Sweden Post created a joint venture in the express delivery market called Vasagatan 11 International AB. The U.S. Postal Service and Federal Express have also formed a joint venture.

Acquisitions of private firms by government postal operators have become common with the liberalization of postal markets. Deutsche Post World Net embarked on a substantial program of mergers and acquisitions after privatization. It acquired a major stake in the international express company DHL in 1998. Similarly, in 1991, the Dutch post office, PTT Post, joined with the post offices of France, Germany, the Netherlands, Canada, and Sweden to purchase 50 percent of the Australian transportation conglomerate TNT. In August 1996, PTT Post acquired complete control of the joint venture operations by purchasing TNT itself.

The subsidies, privileges, and immunities discussed above also allow the government firm to artificially pay more for acquisitions, which can distort market structure. To the extent that the government firm maximizes size, it will be willing to pay more for an acquisition that allows it to expand into other businesses. That is inefficient because the price paid for the acquisition will not reflect its true resource cost.

There are other ways in which special privileges allow a government firm to compete inefficiently. For example, the mailbox monopoly in the United States has important effects in reducing competition and thus assisting in the acquisition of additional rents for the USPS. It raises the costs to rivals of competing with the Postal Service because they may not leave material in the customer's mailbox. It discourages other firms, such as utilities, from integrating into mail delivery because they may be loath to establish their own messenger services. Indeed, discouraging such competition was the original reason for the creation of the mailbox monopoly in 1936.[9] The monopoly also discourages customers from using alternate delivery services because they must install an additional mail receptacle to receive such deliveries.

Case Studies of Competition between Government and Private Firms

In this section, I review seven examples of competition between government and private firms. In each case, I present relevant historical background and institutional detail. I also catalog privileges and immunities government firms enjoy as a result of their special status. I then discuss the nature of the competition between the two entities.

Freight Carried by Passenger Rail

The Rail Passenger Service Act of 1970 created the National Railroad Passenger Corporation, or Amtrak (short for *American travel by track*) in the wake of the Penn Central bankruptcy.[10] Amtrak was established "to provide fast . . . modern, efficient, intercity rail passenger service."[11]

Amtrak enjoys a number of government-granted privileges and immunities. First, although the 1970 act authorized Amtrak to issue common and preferred stock, it has never done so. It remains a state-owned enterprise benefiting from captive equity. Second, it has a government-granted monopoly over intercity railroad passenger service in the lower 48 states. It has used that monopoly power to block entry.

Third, Amtrak benefits from the lack of a bankruptcy constraint. Although it was originally created as a for-profit enterprise and was expected swiftly to become profitable, it has never earned a profit. The General Accounting Office stated that "Amtrak spends almost $2 for every dollar of revenue it earns in providing intercity passenger rail service."[12] Cumulative losses for Amtrak as of 1997 were $13 billion.[13] Such losses would have bankrupted a private firm.

Fourth, Amtrak receives direct government subsidies to defray its capital and operating costs. For example, it received $2 billion in capital funds from Congress in 1999 to modernize its operations, increase productivity, and create new revenue. It received $521 million in direct subsidies each year from 2000 through 2002. Its total lifetime subsidies in 2002 dollars exceeded $44 billion.

Amtrak also received government-granted subsidies through the 1970 act in the form of mandated payments from private railroads. Private railroads were required to make specified payments to Amtrak before they were allowed to discontinue their unprofitable intercity passenger services.[14]

Fifth, Amtrak has the power to force freight railroads to allow it to use their tracks.[15] Amtrak trains take precedence over freight trains when it uses their tracks, making that power even more valuable. It does not pay for the delay costs imposed on freight railroads. Finally, Amtrak is exempt from state and local taxes. It is subject to corporate income tax in theory but has never earned a profit and thus has never paid that tax.

Amtrak is obviously under severe budgetary pressure, and that has encouraged it to venture into new activities. As the *Wall Street Journal* reports, "The railroad (Amtrak), which is partly subsidized by Congress, has been struggling for years with mounting debt and losses and has been looking for new ways to generate revenue."[16] Consistent with theoretical predictions, it has ventured into competitive activities outside of its core service of intercity passenger rail. In 1998, over the objections of competitors such as Union Pacific Corporation, it won approval from the Surface Transportation Board to carry freight on its passenger trains. To initiate its new express freight venture, Amtrak leased 500 freight cars and express vehicles and opened cargo terminals. It began to carry fruit juice, magazines, tuna fish, apples, machinery parts, paper, beer, auto parts, and other goods on freight cars attached to its passenger trains. It also started carrying California tomatoes and Florida oranges and ventured into same-day express package delivery on its Metroliner service between New York and Washington, D.C.

That expansion into freight carriage competed not only with private freight railroads but also with trucking companies. Although potential customers wanted the program expanded into their regions, trucking companies were concerned. Scott Woods, director of national accounts for Dick Simon Trucking, Inc., stated, "This is a competitive industry that Amtrak should stay out of . . . Amtrak's business is moving people, not produce."[17]

Amtrak worked actively to expand its freight service both by increasing service on some routes and by adding new routes. Some long-haul trains ended up carrying more freight than people, and Amtrak started adding new trains based on expected revenue from express freight service.[18] It also expressed interest in operating between Chicago and Portland a new freight-carrying train that would have used Union Pacific's tracks.

Although Amtrak ultimately decided to end its express freight service in 2002, this episode suggests that SOEs will enter new, competitive lines of business to find additional sources of revenue.

Financial Services

The Federal Reserve System is the central bank of the United States. It was created by Congress in 1913 to provide the nation with a stable monetary and financial system. The Federal Reserve (the Fed) summarizes its duties as "(1) conducting the nation's monetary policy; (2) supervising and regulating banking institutions and protecting the credit rights of consumers; (3) maintaining the stability of the financial system; and (4) providing certain financial services to the U.S. government, the public, financial institutions, and foreign official institutions."[19]

Regarding the fourth task, the Fed provides to member banks various financial payment services including check clearing, wire transfers, automated clearinghouse transfers, securities safekeeping, currency processing, and settlement. The provision of payment services placed the Fed in direct competition with large commercial banks and clearinghouses.[20] The Federal Reserve System's reaction to the Monetary Control Act of 1980 provides insights into the behavior of government firms when they enter competitive activities.

Before the Monetary Control Act, Federal Reserve Banks were not required to recover the cost of providing those services through fees. Payment services were provided at no charge to member banks, whereas nonmember banks were not given access to the services. Under the 1980 act, the Fed was to ensure that all major services it supplied were explicitly priced.

The act required that the fees charged for Fed services be based on all the direct and indirect costs incurred by the Federal Reserve. The fees were also to include the *imputed costs of taxes* and *the return on capital* the Fed would have to pay if it were privately owned.[21] Those requirements are noteworthy because they explicitly recognize in law that exemption from taxes and from paying a return on capital to investors create unfair advantages to SOEs in areas in which they compete. The act required that float be priced at the federal funds rate. The Fed was also required to reduce budgets commensurately when demand for services fell as fees increased. Fee revenue reverted to the Treasury.

As a result, the Fed lost market share. The market share for its check processing business, for example, fell from 43 percent before the act to 33 percent in 1983.[22] The Fed reduced staff because of the decreased check-clearing volume.[23]

Competing commercial banks argued that the Fed, concerned about those losses, began understating its costs where it faced intense competition. As Charles Bates of the American Bankers Association stated, the reason they understated costs was "because their share of market was falling. They were going to have to cut their staffs. What they have done is clearly predatory—and you can put my name on that and blaze it all over Washington."[24] The Fed responded that it was not understating its costs but that its fees were low because of enhanced efficiency.

Ken Cavalluzzo, Christopher Ittner, and David Larker conducted a formal econometric analysis of the effects of the Monetary Control Act.[25] Their results address the disagreement. They found that the Fed reacted to the act both by improving its efficiency and by reallocating some of its indirect costs to less competitive activities. They also found that overhead costs decreased in competitive, priced activities but increased in other activities consistent with at least some indirect costs being reallocated from more competitive to less competitive activities.

There are several lessons in this episode. First, it suggests that below-cost pricing of government-provided services indeed crowds out private firms. The pricing of check-clearing services, for example, led to the entry or expansion of 95 local check-clearing associations.[26] Second, the Fed responded to the Monetary Control Act by reallocating some indirect costs from priced to nonpriced services. If that evidence and the commercial bank's arguments are correct, then, consistent with Sappington and Sidak's theory, the Fed was attempting to maintain market share by depressing prices at which it faces competition.

Water Utilities

The water utility industry provides an instructive historical example of direct competition between government and private firms. There was a wave of municipal acquisitions of private water companies in the United States between 1880 and 1930.[27] City governments wanted to acquire the waterworks at least cost and employed a range of strategies to get private water companies to reduce their asking prices.

Some cities secured passage of state laws allowing them to acquire water companies through the power of eminent domain.[28] Others used their regulatory powers to undermine the value of private enterprises. In Kansas City, local politicians used a tortured interpretation of a phrase in a private water company's franchise as a pretext for seizing the company's plant and distribution system without offering any compensation.[29]

However, the most common strategy employed by cities to get private companies to reduce their asking price was to construct competing public waterworks. Some private water companies sued for injunctive relief, and courts expressed unease about competing municipal waterworks. Echoing concerns about competition between government and private firms today, the Supreme Court noted that competition from "the city may be far more destructive than that of a private company" because the city could conduct its "business without regard to profit" and "resort to public taxation to make up for losses."[30]

A handful of state and federal judges believed that competition from municipal waterworks violated private water companies' rights to substantive due process, in effect depriving private companies of their property without "just compensation or due process of law." In a dissent to a decision by the New York Supreme Court that allowed a municipal water company to enter into competition with a private company, Justice Bartlett wrote, "[I]t is obvious that the municipal water company is in no legal sense the ordinary competitor of the old company, but is armed with powers that will inevitably drive the latter from the field, and its bondholders and stockholders be subjected to a total loss of all capital invested." According to Bartlett, this "is not competition; it is annihilation."[31]

To some extent, private water companies anticipated that behavior and often demanded provisions in their franchises limiting the authority of local governments to regulate, tax, and construct competing enterprises. The problem with such contractual provisions, however, is that they were often either unenforceable or interpreted in unforeseeable ways. For example, the courts ruled that, as corporations chartered by the state, cities could not contract away their powers to regulate and tax, regardless of the franchises they granted to private water companies. Hence, if a state legislature empowered a local government with the authority to regulate water rates, the municipality could not forsake that power in a contract; only the state could revoke such power.

Moreover, the courts were bound to interpret ambiguous or unclear franchise provisions against the franchisee (the private water company) and in favor of the local government. In the words of the Supreme Court, "grants of franchises and special privileges are always to be construed most strongly against the donee, and in favor of the public."[32]

The impact of that interpretive principle is illustrated by a case in which a city included in the franchise of a private water company a provision promising that the city would, under no circumstances, "grant to any other person or corporation" the privilege of furnishing water to the city. Twenty years later, when the city in question built its own waterworks to compete with that same private water company, the private company sued for injunctive relief. Ruling against the company, the Supreme Court held that the franchise merely implied that the city did not have the right to build a competing works. Apparently, the phrase *any other person or corporation* might or might not have included the city.[33]

The water utility example also reveals the efficiency cost of competition from government firms, particularly due to underinvestment. There is evidence that private water companies facing a high risk of municipal takeover refused to extend water mains or build water filtration systems without additional promises from city authorities that they would not be taken over or that they would at least be adequately compensated if taken over.[34]

In some states, private water companies lobbied for, and secured passage of, required-purchase laws. Those laws compelled towns to buy private water companies already in operation before they built their own waterworks. Although courts in a few states struck down required-purchase laws as unconstitutional infringements on the power of local governments, the state courts that upheld them viewed required-purchase laws as mechanisms to promote private investment and development of the water industry in general.[35]

Upholding a required-purchase law in Pennsylvania, the state supreme court clearly articulated its concerns about underinvestment by private firms in the face of government competition: "A municipality, in its beginnings, is perhaps not financially strong, or its debt may approach the constitutional limit so closely that it cannot borrow. Nevertheless the low state of its financial condition does not render less urgent the necessity of water supply. It can obtain it in but one way—by contract with those who have the money, and are willing to invest their private capital in the construction of waterworks. The legislature knew that capital would not be invested in such an enterprise if in the future it were liable to confiscation by competition with a public enterprise operated from a municipal treasury capable of replenishment from the pocket of the taxpayer."[36]

Electric Utilities

Government is heavily involved in the electric power industry. Federal government involvement in electricity occurs through the Alaska Power Administration, the Bonneville Power Authority (BPA), the Southeastern Power Administration, the Southwestern Power Administration, the Western Area Power Administration, and the Tennessee Valley Authority (TVA). There are also state power projects, such as the Salt River Project in Arizona.

I focus on the TVA because of its massive size. The TVA is America's largest wholesale supplier of electricity, marketing about one-half of total federal power production. It operates 113 hydroelectric units, 59 coal-fired units, and 5 working nuclear units. It provides about seven million people in Tennessee, Mississippi, Alabama, Kentucky, North Carolina, Virginia, and Georgia with electricity service.

The TVA was created in 1933 to assist the South during the Great Depression. Its mission was to "strengthen the regional economy by supplying low-cost power" to the region.[37] In addition to electric power development, President Franklin Roosevelt envisioned that the TVA would also control flooding, modernize farming, and attract industry.

In 1959, a federal law was passed that required the TVA's power program to become self-financing through revenues from electricity sales, and the TVA has not received direct government payments for its power-related activities since that time.[38] The law also allowed the TVA to pay for its plants and transmission lines through the issuance of bonds.

The TVA enjoys a number of government-granted privileges and immunities. First, it is government owned. Its taxpayer-owners are disallowed from selling their equity stake in the firm or from acquiring additional equity. Thus, the TVA does not have to pay those owners an expected return; it benefits from captive equity.

Second, the TVA's enormous debt carries an implicit government guarantee, which significantly lowers it costs. The TVA has incurred debt of over $29 billion, just within the statutory limit of $30 billion. Importantly, its bonds are considered to be government securities and are exempt from registration under the Securities Act of 1933. For example, the General Accounting Office noted that

> The TVA Act states that the federal government does not guarantee TVA's bonds . . . because TVA is a wholly owned government corporation, there is the perception in the investment community, including two credit rating firms we contacted (Moody's Investors Service and Standard & Poor's), that the federal government would support principal and interest payments on TVA debt if TVA's solvency were to be seriously impaired. Because they believe that the federal government would intercede to protect TVA's solvency, the two credit rating firms we contacted perceive that there is an implicit government guarantee of TVA bonds. . . . Of the 119 electric utilities rated by one of the firms as of October 2000, TVA was the only utility rated Aaa. The high bond ratings result in lower interest expense for TVA, which in turn reduces its fixed annual operating expense. According to our analysis, as a result of its high bond ratings, the annual interest expense on TVA's bonds outstanding at September 30, 2000, would have been between $137 million and $245 million higher (about 2 to 4 percent of fiscal year 2000 total expenses) if TVA's bond ratings were lower.[39]

In addition to the subsidy to the TVA's debt from an implicit government guarantee, TVA debt holders do not pay state or local taxes on interest from the TVA's debt. Lenders are thus willing to accept a lower rate of interest to hold that debt.

Third, the TVA pays no state or federal income taxes. In lieu of taxes, it makes payments to state and local governments equal to 5 percent of its revenues from power sales to nonfederal agencies. Fourth, it is exempt from hundreds of federal and state regulations and is immune from antitrust laws.[40]

Finally, there are a variety of other idiosyncratic benefits that the

TVA receives because of its government status. For example, in 1998 it refinanced a \$3.2 billion loan from the federal government. The loan carried a prepayment penalty, but Congress retroactively changed the loan's terms to exempt the TVA from the penalty.[41]

The TVA's use of government-granted privileges and immunities has given rise to multifarious anticompetitive concerns. One is in its own core area of providing electricity. Although the TVA enjoys a monopoly in its main service area, it faces competition on the margins of its service territory. It competes aggressively to retain customers on those margins.

An instructive example involves the municipally owned electric power distribution system in Bristol, Virginia, which serves about 12,000 customers. Consistent with the Federal Energy Policy Act of 1992, Bristol entered the power market in an attempt to lower its costs and received bids from 19 prospective energy suppliers. The TVA's bid was the least competitive. Bristol was able to reduce its power costs by one-third relative to the TVA's rates by entering into a seven-year contract to purchase power from an investor-owned utility, Cinergy Services, starting January 1, 1998.

In retaliation, the TVA engaged in overtly distortionary pricing.[42] It attempted to reclaim Bristol's large industrial customers by sending them letters stating that "TVA would propose to serve your plant . . . firm power indexed to be 2% less than BVUB's (Bristol Virginia Utilities Board's) legitimate published firm rates."[43] The TVA was thus offering to reduce its price to 2 percent below Bristol's price, regardless of its costs and regardless of what that price might be.

The TVA proceeded to threaten to withhold access to the electrical interchange facilities Bristol needed to be able to exchange emergency power with its sister city of Bristol, Tennessee.[44] The TVA also demanded that Bristol pay it the exorbitant sum of \$54.1 million to offset stranded investment costs even though the TVA knew many years before that Bristol was searching for a new supplier and thus could have easily avoided those costs through planning.

Finally, in a thinly veiled threat, the TVA's Chairman, Craven Crowell, wrote a letter to the mayor of Bristol on January 10, 1997, suggesting that the Bristol community was likely to suffer from blackouts if it purchased power from an alternative supplier. Those actions would likely raise the curiosity of antitrust enforcement agencies if undertaken by a nongovernment firm.

In a representative example of SOE behavior, the TVA incurred enormous debt through poor management, inaccurate demand forecasting, excessive investment in nuclear plants, and an unwillingness to increase rates. The resulting financial difficulties inspired the TVA to consider seeking more revenue by expanding into new, competitive activities, including cable television and telecommunications.[45]

The TVA's chairman, however, took the additional step of hinting at a taxpayer-funded bailout if Congress was not mindful of the TVA's needs, stating that "If Congress does anything that devalues us, you always have the potential for the Treasury having to get involved."[46] That speaks to the strategic value to the SOE of not facing a bankruptcy constraint.

The TVA example illustrates that an SOE is able and willing to use its government-granted subsidies and privileges to behave anticompetitively in those areas in which it faces competition and to seek new revenues by entering supplementary lines of business.

Weather Forecasting

The National Weather Service (NWS) is a federal agency under the National Oceanic and Atmospheric Administration (NOAA), which is part of the United States Department of Commerce. Its annual expenditures are around $700 million.[47] The legislative authority allowing government provision of weather services was granted through the Organic Act of 1890.[48]

The National Weather Service's mission, as stated in the Organic Act, is to protect life and property and to enhance the national economy. Given that weather-related damages in the United States total about $20 billion per year, that is a significant responsibility.[49] The NWS accomplishes its mission through two core activities. First, it provides forecasts and warnings of severe weather, flooding, and hurricanes. It issues aviation forecasts for airports and produces daily fire weather forecasts and marine forecasts for coastal locations. It is the only entity that can offer official severe storm warnings.

Second, it collects and distributes basic meteorological and climatic data. Surface and upper air data are gathered routinely. It uses satellite imagery to assist in forecasting and radar imagery to assist in issuing severe weather warnings. It also operates NOAA Weather Radio (which has hundreds of transmitters located across the nation) as well as various centers, such as the Storm Prediction Center, the National Hurricane Center, and the National Climatic Data Center.

In recent decades, weather forecasting services in the United States have evolved from being almost exclusively government provided into a combination of government, private, and nonprofit provision. Private weather forecasting is a large, thriving industry in the United States.[50] The National Weather Service reports web sites for 269 commercial weather vendors.[51] Private forecasting firms now provide more than 85 percent of the total weather forecasts in the country.

Private firms offer customized forecasts, tailoring them to specific business needs, and clients pay for forecasts. Some companies use the raw data collected by the National Weather Service as input into proprietary weather forecast models. Private weather firms also provide clients with computer hardware and software, observational systems, imaging systems, displays, and charts. The NWS has competed in many of those same areas, often providing similar services for free.

In 1991, the NWS issued a policy statement entitled "The National Weather Service (NWS) and the Private Weather Industry: A Public-Private Partnership." A key provision of the policy statement says that "The NWS will not compete with the private sector when a service is currently provided by commercial enterprises, unless otherwise directed by applicable law."[52] That provision has not been maintained consistently, however. The NWS in some instances has declined to discontinue competing with private firms, citing the 1890 Organic Act.[53]

Commentators have noted that government competition in weather forecasting may force private firms out of the industry at taxpayers' expense. In 1989, Jerome Ellig observed, "Clearly, if a government weather bureau providing commercial services charges its clients less than the incremental costs of those services, private firms will find it extremely difficult to compete, even if they receive all of the government's weather data for free. In this case, private firms are obviously competing against a taxpayer-subsidized bureaucracy. Some firms that could provide forecasts less expensively, or more accurately, get pushed out of the market. Taxpayers pay a higher bill for the weather bureaucracy, and they get fewer or less useful or less accurate forecasts to boot."[54]

Regarding investment, Rolland Hauser, a professor of geoscience at California State University, stated that "Current federal ag-weather policy, either advertently or inadvertently, has the effect of deterring investment by private meteorology in agricultural weather services."[55] Similarly, Jeffrey Smith, director of the Association of Private Weather Related Companies, stated that "Many commercial meteorologists have been reluctant to take an increased role in forecasting because of the constant threat of government provision of these specialized forecasting services. Private firms do not know what service the government may choose to offer next for 'free.'"[56] The case of weather forecasting suggests the importance of formulating a clear policy with regard to competition between government and private firms. It also illustrates the dynamics of such competition as the private sector evolves to fill new market needs.

The Provision of Information

The National Technical Information Service (NTIS) is a small agency within the Department of Commerce. It was created in 1950 to serve as a clearinghouse within the government for the collection and dissemination of information. Its core mission is to collect, organize, sort, and disseminate government scientific, technical, and engineering information. The NTIS was to be financially self-sustaining, that is, to break even over time, and it charges customers for documents in its clearinghouse. It is thus similar to a state-owned enterprise. Until the late 1980s, the NTIS received a direct appropriation from Congress.

The NTIS's revenue has consistently declined because former customers are now able to download over the Internet documents they would have previously purchased from the NTIS. Its revenue declined 18 percent between 1993 and 1998, and the number of documents it sold also declined.[57] As the model of SOE behavior predicts, the NTIS began to seek new sources of revenue by venturing into competitive activities. Deputy Secretary of Commerce Robert Mallett stated

> It is important to note that, to offset losses, NTIS has significantly changed its business mix. Over half of its revenues are now derived from services provided to other government agencies, up from one-third only five years ago. NTIS has also ventured into other business products; one example is producing and selling a CD-ROM of IRS tax forms. Revenues from NTIS' other business lines in FY 1999 have offset Clearinghouse losses and has allowed the organization to show a profit. But, as the Department's IG (Inspector General) stated earlier this year, "We are also concerned that in order to replace lost sales, NTIS is seeking business opportunities on the perimeter of its statutory mission, where it risks competing against private businesses." Others, including Members of Congress, have raised similar concerns.[58]

Additionally, the NTIS announced a partnership with Northern Light, a private firm. The partnership would have created a fee-based Internet search engine for government documents. Northern Light and the NTIS would have split income fees. The Clinton Administration, however, concluded that the NTIS should withdraw from the venture and that Northern Light should continue on its own.[59] The NTIS example indicates that agencies within government are also likely to behave in an anticompetitive manner when faced with a budget constraint.

Marine Towing Services

The nonemergency marine services industry suggests a successful policy approach to competition between government and private firms. The implementation of policies protecting private firms from government competition can save taxpayers substantial sums and allow private commerce to expand. Competition between the Coast Guard and private firms for nonemergency boat towing offers an example.

For many years, the Coast Guard provided nonemergency towing services to boat owners (e.g., those out of gas or aground on a sand bar) at no charge. A 1983 law prohibited the Coast Guard from competing with private firms providing those services. Private marine assistance firms include Sea Tow, Vessel Assist, and Safe/Sea, among others. To comply with the law, the Coast Guard observed a rule whereby it would give private firms preference in assisting a boater in need of nonemergency aid. The Coast Guard would respond only if a private firm could not assist within one hour.

This law has facilitated a dramatic expansion of the marine assistance industry. When the 1983 law was passed, there were fewer than ten private marine assistance firms in the United States. There are currently more than 300 such firms. Customers can buy annual towing insurance memberships, modeled on the American Automobile Association.[60]

The law has also resulted in savings for taxpayers. The annual caseload of the Coast Guard dropped from about 81,000 in 1983 to approximately 47,000 in 1999, despite the fact that there was a marked increase in the number of registered boats during that period. This was due in large part to the rise of private towing services. The reduction has allowed the Coast Guard to allocate its scarce resources to crucial core activities such as marine safety and emergency rescue. It has also placed the cost of nonemergency aid on those using the service, thus enhancing fairness and providing incentives for boaters to take proper precautions.

Summary and Conclusions

Government firms potentially benefit from a number of subsidies, privileges, and immunities not normally granted to private firms. These include monopoly power, credit guarantees, freedom from paying investors an expected rate of return, exemption from bankruptcy, tax exemptions, direct subsidies, and immunity from antitrust prosecution, disclosure requirements, and other regulations. There are also a variety of privileges and immunities that are specific to particular SOEs and GSEs. Where a government firm competes with a private firm, it can use those advantages to diminish or eliminate a rival not enjoying the same benefits.

Government firms, particularly those facing budgetary constraints, have an incentive to search for new sources of revenue. They can secure that revenue by venturing into activities where private firms already operate. However, a government firm, absent its various subsidies, privileges, and immunities, may be higher cost than its private rivals but still able to force those rivals from the market or deter their entry. In cases in which government and private firms compete, more efficient private rivals may reduce their endeavors, or they may be loath to invest in new activities where there is significant government competition or uncertainty about future government competition. Or they may be unwilling to enter the market at all.

Competition between government and private firms in both core and noncore business areas is pervasive. The examples of competition between government and private firms surveyed in this chapter include freight carried by passenger rail, financial services, water utilities, electric utilities, weather forecasting, provision of information, and marine towing services. But there are many others such as the government-sponsored enterprises Fannie Mae and Freddie Mac that compete in automated underwriting, as discussed in Chapter 3.

Notes

1. See, e.g., R. Braeutigan and J. Panzar, "Diversification Incentives Under 'Price-Based' and 'Cost-Based' Regulation," *Rand Journal of Regulation* 20, no. 3 (autumn 1989): 373–91; T. Brennan, "Cross-Subsidization and Cost Misallocation by Regulated Monopolists," *Journal of Regulatory Economics* 2, no. 1 (March 1990): 37–51; and G. Sweeny, "Welfare Implications of Fully Distributed Cost Pricing Applied to Partially Regulated Firms," *Bell Journal of Economics* 13, no. 2 (autumn 1982): 525–33.

2. W. P. Rogerson, "Overhead Allocation and Incentives for Cost Minimization in Defense Procurement," *The Accounting Review* 67, no. 4 (October 1992): 671–90.

3. D. Dranove, "Pricing by Non-Profit Institutions: The Case of Hospital Cost-Shifting," *Journal of Health Economics* 7, no. 1 (March 1988): 47–57; and R. W. Foster, "Cost-Shifting Under Cost-Reimbursement and Prospective Payment," *Journal of Health Economics* 4, no. 3 (September 1985): 261–71.

4. For brevity, I here use the term *government firm* to refer to any firm receiving special government-granted privileges and immunities (including government-sponsored enterprises) as opposed to government-owned firms.

5. Paul W. MacAvoy and George S. McIssac, "The Current File on the Case for Privatization of the Federal Government Enterprises," in *Deregulation and Privatization in the United States, Hume Papers on Public Policy* 3, ed. Paul W. MacAvoy (Edinburgh: Edinburgh University Press 1995).

6. See John R. Lott Jr., *Are Predatory Commitments Credible? Who Should the Courts Believe?* (Chicago: University of Chicago Press, 1999).

7. Michael A. Crew and Paul R. Kleindorfer, "Privatizing the U.S. Postal Service," in *Mail @ the Millennium*, ed. Edward L. Hudgins (Washington, D.C.: Cato Institute, 2000), 155.

8. The Postal Service's antitrust immunity is being questioned in the courts. See *Flamingo Industries (USA) Ltd v. U.S. Postal Service*, 302 F.3d 985, 988–89 (9th Cir. 2002). The case is being appealed to the Supreme Court.

9. See J. Gregory Sidak and Daniel F. Spulber, *Protecting Competition from the Postal Monopoly* (Washington, D.C.: AEI Press, 1996), 345.

10. Public Law No. 91-518.

11. Rail Passenger Service Act of 1970, Public Law No. 91-518, Sec. 101.

12. U.S. General Accounting Office, *Intercity Passenger Rail: Financial Performance of Amtrak's Routes*, May 1998, 2.

13. Christopher B. Cohen, "Get Amtrak Back on Track," *Wall Street Journal*, 30 April 1997.

14. Michael A. Schuyler, *The Anti-Competitive Edge: Government Subsidies to Government Businesses* (Washington, D.C.: Institute for Research on the Economics of Taxation, 1999), 80, n. 118.

15. U.S. Code, Title 49, Chapter 243. U.S. General Accounting Office, *Intercity Passenger Rail: Financial Performance of Amtrak's Routes*, May 1998, 18–19.

16. Daniel Machalaba, "Amtrak Gets Federal Approval to Carry Express Freight on Its Passenger Trains," *Wall Street Journal*, 1 June 1998, B2.

17. Quoted in Brooks Barnes, "Packers Want Amtrak to Help Ship Apples," *Wall Street Journal*, 19 February 2000, NW1.

18. Daniel Machalaba, "Amtrak Is to End Cargo Service; Operation Had $7 Million Loss," *Wall Street Journal*, 14 October 2002, C7.

19. http://www.federalreserve.gov.

20. See R. Trigaux, "Fed Pricing One Year Later: Banks Wary of New Rival," *American Banker* (17 June 1982): 1.

21. Ken S. Cavalluzzo, Christopher D. Ittner, and David F. Larker, "Competition, Efficiency, and Cost Allocation in Government Agencies: Evidence on the Federal Reserve System," *Journal of Accounting Research* 36, no. 1 (spring 1998): 2.

22. D. B. Humphrey, "Resource Use in Federal Reserve Check and ACH

Operations After Pricing," *Journal of Bank Research* 12 (spring 1985): 45–53.

23. W. F. Ford, "The Changing Role of the Federal Reserve in the Payment System," *Journal of Cash Management* (April/May 1983): 12–19.

24. Martin Mayer, "The Fed Goes into Business," *Fortune* (4 April 1983): 169.

25. Ken S. Cavalluzzo, Christopher D. Ittner, and David F. Larker, "Competition, Efficiency, and Cost Allocation in Government Agencies: Evidence on the Federal Reserve System," *Journal of Accounting Research* 36, no. 1 (spring 1998): 2.

26. This is similar to the expansion of private marine assistance services discussed later in this chapter.

27. See Werner Troesken and Rick Geddes, "The Municipalization of U.S. Waterworks, 1897–1915," *Journal of Law, Economics, and Organization* 19, no. 2 (fall 2003): 373–400, for a discussion of why those acquisitions occurred.

28. See, for example, *Long Island Water Supply Company v. Brooklyn*, 166 U.S. 722 1897 and *City of Leavenworth et. al. v. Leavenworth City and Fort Leavenworth Water Company*, 76 Pac. 451 (Kansas, 1904).

29. See *National Waterworks Company v. Kansas City*, 62 Fed. 853 (1894).

30. *Walla Walla Waterworks v. City of Walla Walla*, 172 U.S. 1 1898, 17–18.

31. See *Skaneateles Waterworks Co. v. Village of Skaneateles, et. al.*, 55 N.E. 562 (1899, New York), especially pp. 567–68.

32. *Knoxville Water Company v. Knoxville*, 200 U.S. 22 1906, 28.

33. *Knoxville Water Company v. Knoxville*, 200 U.S. 22 1906, 33–34 and 36–37.

34. See Troesken and Geddes "The Municipalization of U.S. Waterworks" for further evidence on underinvestment by private water utilities due to competitive threats from municipal utilities.

35. See, for example, *Asbury et. al. v. Town of Albemarle*, 78 S.E. 146 (North Carolina, 1913) and *Helena Consolidated Water Company v. Steele*, 49 Pac. 382 (Montana, 1902).

36. *White et. al. v. City of Meadville*, 35 A. 695 (Pennsylvania 1896), 698.

37. *1997 TVA Annual Report*, 6.

38. It continues to receive subsidies for its non-power-related activities.

39. U.S. General Accounting Office, *Tennessee Valley Authority: Bond Ratings Based on Ties to the Federal Government and Other Nonfinancial Factors*, April 2001 (GAO-01–540), 2–3.

40. See Richard Munson, "Restructure TVA: Why the Tennessee Valley Authority Must Be Reformed" (2001), available at http://www.nemw .org/ERtva_reform.htm.

41. Michael A. Schuyler, *The Anti-Competitive Edge: Government Subsidies to Government Businesses* (Washington, D.C.: Institute for Research on the Economics of Taxation, 1999), 67–68.

42. Although it is tempting to call this pricing predatory, that implies the firm will raise its price in the future to recoup its losses from pricing below cost now. Because they are not profit maximizers, SOEs do not need to recoup losses in the future.

43. W. *David Fletcher's Statement to be Presented to United States House of Representatives Committee on the Judiciary Oversight Hearing on 'The Application of the Anti-Trust Laws to the Tennessee Valley Authority and the Federal Power Marketing Administrations' on October 22, 1997.* Available at http://www.house.gov/judiciary/1093.htm.

44. Ibid.

45. Jeffrey Ball, "TVA Plan Seen by Critics as Unfair Grab for Power," *Wall Street Journal*, 5 March 1997, S1.

46. Ibid.

47. See http://www.srh.noaa.gov/bna/vision.html.

48. 15 U.S.C 9 §313.

49. See *Fair Weather: Effective Partnerships in Weather and Climate Services* (Washington, D.C.: National Research Council, 2003), prepublication version, executive summary.

50. Jerome Ellig, *Government and the Weather: The Privatization Option*, Reason Foundation Issue Paper no. 109 (August 1989).

51. See http://205.156.54.206/im/more.htm

52. See *Federal Register*, 56, no. 13, Friday, 18 January 1991, p. 1985.

53. See Michael S. Leavitt, "Testimony of the Commercial Weather Services Association by Michael S. Leavitt, President, Weather Services Corporation, Before the Subcommittee on Energy and Environment, U.S. House of Representatives, April 9, 1997," available at http:// www.house.gov/science/leavitt_4-9.html.

54. Jerome Ellig, *Government and the Weather*, 10.

55. Rolland K. Hauser, *The Interface Between Federal and Commercial Weather Services for Agricultural Industries—A Question of Policy*, report prepared for the U.S. Department of Commerce, National Oce-

anic and Atmospheric Administration, Office of the Administrator (November 1985), 42.

56. Jeffrey C. Smith, "Private and Public Roles in Weather Forecasting in the United States," (August 1988), 2.

57. Department of Commerce, A *Report on the National Technical Information Service (NTIS)*, fall 1999.

58. Robert Mallett, *Testimony of Robert Mallett, Deputy Secretary of Commerce, Before the Subcommittee on Science, Technology, and Space, Committee on Commerce, Science and Transportation, United States Senate,* 21 October 1999.

59. Joseph E. Stiglitz, Peter R. Orszag, and Jonathan M. Orszag, *The Role of Government in a Digital Age*, Study Commissioned by the Computer & Communications Industry Association (October 2000), 115.

60. See *Privatization of Coast Guard Marine Assistance Service*, available at http://www.c-port.org/resources/privatization.html.

Chapter 3

Applying the Microsoft Decision to Fannie Mae and Freddie Mac

Peter J. Wallison

The unanimous decision of the United States Court of Appeals for the D.C. Circuit, on June 28, 2001, affirming major elements of the original Microsoft decision, provides a template for analyzing the activities of Fannie Mae and Freddie Mac under the antitrust laws.[1] Using the court's analysis, a strong case can be made that Fannie and Freddie are monopolizing the automated underwriting market in violation of Section 2 of the Sherman Act and attempting to monopolize both the automated underwriting market and at least one other mortgage finance–related market.[2] There is also a strong case that the GSEs have tied their automated underwriting services to their monopoly in the secondary mortgage market, which would be a per se violation of Section 1 of the Sherman Act.[3] However, there is as yet no available public information that the GSEs are illegally tying other products and services to their automated underwriting systems.

Fannie Mae and Freddie Mac

Fannie Mae (the Federal National Mortgage Association) and Freddie Mac (the Federal Home Loan Mortgage Corporation) are two government-chartered corporations initially created for the purpose of increasing the liquidity of the residential mortgage market. They perform this function by purchasing residential mortgages from banks for their portfolios or by guaranteeing securities based on pools of mortgages assembled by lenders or other mortgage originators. Through different routes, both companies were partially privatized—Fannie in 1968 and Freddie in the mid-1980s—and both are now owned entirely by shareholders and listed on the New York Stock Exchange.

Nevertheless, the terms of their partial privatization left both companies with special privileges and links to the government so that, despite their private ownership, they are known as Government-Sponsored Enterprises, or GSEs. To distinguish them from other corporations with government support, they are sometimes called the Housing GSEs. In this chapter, I refer to them simply as Fannie and Freddie or, together, as the GSEs.

The special links to the federal government are numerous and very important. For example,

- The President appoints five members (a minority) of their boards of directors.
- They are exempt from state and local taxes.
- Their securities are exempt from registration with the Securities and Exchange Commission, although both have voluntarily agreed to file reports with the SEC under the Securities Exchange Act of 1934.
- They each have a so-called line of credit at the Treasury under which the Secretary of the Treasury is authorized to invest up to $2.25 billion in their securities.

- Their securities are eligible for unlimited investment by national banks and as collateral for Treasury tax accounts deposited with banks.

These and other ties to the federal government, along with the fact that they are performing a government mission, have apparently convinced the financial markets that the government will not allow the GSEs to fail. This implied government backing, in turn, enables them to borrow money at interest rates that are significantly lower than any private sector AAA credit and only slightly more than the Treasury itself is required to pay. With this superior financing ability, the GSEs have been able completely to dominate the secondary market for conventional/conforming residential mortgages (mortgages of less than $322,700 in 2003), which constitute roughly 70 percent of all residential mortgages in the United States.[4] They now hold in portfolio, or have guaranteed, mortgages or mortgage-backed securities (MBS) representing about 75 percent of all conventional/conforming mortgages, and Bert Ely and I have estimated, in a monograph published in 2000, that those two companies will hold, or have guaranteed, securities representing almost 50 percent of all mortgages in the United States by the end of 2003.[5]

The implied government backing for the GSEs has a tangible value recently estimated by the Congressional Budget Office (CBO) at $10.7 billion during 2000. According to the CBO, about 37 percent of this subsidy is retained by the GSEs, enhancing the value of their shares and increasing management compensation; the balance is passed along to the mortgage market in the form of somewhat lower interest rates. Economic studies have shown that the interest rates on mortgages purchased or guaranteed by the GSEs are about 25 to 30 basis points lower than the rates on mortgages above the conventional/conforming loan limit of $322,700. Accordingly, in the competitive residential mortgage market, it is essential that a lender be able to resell a mortgage to one of the GSEs, and thus virtually all conventional/conforming mortgages—which means virtually all middle class mortgages with principal amounts less than the $322,700 loan limit—conform to standards established by the GSEs.

Automated Underwriting Systems

Recently, advances in data processing technology have permitted the development of predictive models of creditworthiness. Those models use correlations among various data elements to predict the likelihood of default by a borrower. Although the models are relatively new and have not been tested in a serious economic downturn, they have assumed great importance in the credit industry. For one thing, they significantly reduce both the cost and time associated with underwriting a credit, enabling lenders to shorten response times on loan applications and reduce interest rates. When applied to the residential mortgage market, automated underwriting, or AU, has become an essential competitive tool. For obvious reasons, a mortgage lender cannot effectively compete for residential mortgage business unless it can offer the reduced interest rates and rapid response times that have been made possible by AU.

Because the GSEs purchase mortgages from banks and other lenders, they have developed their own AU systems. The systems are competitive with and can substitute for similar systems developed by mortgage lenders and mortgage insurers. The GSEs' systems are also proprietary; mortgage lenders do not know whether a mortgage will be accepted or rejected by the GSEs' AU systems until they have been run through.

This is not to say that the GSEs will reject all mortgages that are not approved by their systems; they will accept such mortgages but with much more stringent representations and with warranties that place greater risk on the lender. For example, under certain circumstances, a lender may have to repurchase a mortgage from the GSEs if it was not approved by the GSEs' AU systems and subsequently defaults. In addition, the GSEs offer their AU systems bundled with other services and software that competitive AU systems cannot match, or they offer their systems at discounts that again undersell independent systems available in the market.

Finally, for certain kinds of high loan-to-value (LTV) mortgages, the GSEs will only accept mortgages that meet their AU standards, so lenders for these popular mortgages are required to use the GSEs' systems unless they want to hold the loans in their own portfolios. This creates a degree of liquidity risk because the loans cannot at a later time be sold to the GSEs or to other financial institutions that are assembling loans for a GSE guarantee.

But the strongest inducement to use the GSEs' AU systems is the fact that it is the most effective way of assuring that a mortgage loan will be purchased by one of the GSEs, thus reducing the lender's cost or risk of carrying the loan. And because the GSEs are, as a result of their government support, the sole economically feasible purchasers of the vast majority of all conventional/conforming mortgage loans made in the United States, lenders that use the GSEs' AU systems gain considerable cost advantages over lenders that do not. It is of course possible that a lender might develop its own AU system or purchase an AU system from an independent developer and use that system to evaluate its loans, but this would represent a higher cost initially, as well as assumption of costly risks in selling the loan to the GSEs.

As early as February 1999, Morgan Stanley estimated that the GSEs' combined market share in the use of AU by lenders was 95 percent and likely to grow. As a Morgan Stanley analyst said in a report on the GSEs' technology developments, "[W]e believe that automated underwriting systems, of the sort developed by Fannie Mae and Freddie Mac . . . , constitute a kind of 'killer app' for the mortgage sector."[6]

The Microsoft Decision

In its Microsoft decision, the D.C. Circuit confronted Microsoft's use of another killer app—the Windows operating system. The government claimed that Microsoft was monopolizing the market for personal computer operating systems, attempting to monopolize the Internet browser market, and illegally tying other products to the Windows operating system. The trial court found for the government on all three claims, and Microsoft appealed.[7]

In its decision, the court affirmed the district court in part and reversed in part, ultimately holding that Microsoft had violated Section 2 of the Sherman Act by employing anticompetitive means to maintain its monopoly in the operating system market, reversing the district court's finding that Microsoft had attempted to monopolize the browser market, and remanding for further proceedings the question of whether Microsoft had violated Section 1 of the Sherman Act by tying its Internet browser to the Windows operating system. Microsoft subsequently settled the case with the Department of Justice, but the analysis of a unanimous D.C. Circuit Court of Appeals is still a valid template for assessing the GSEs' use of automated underwriting under antitrust laws. The following is a summary of the circuit court's analysis in each major category.

Monopolization

The court noted [quoting *United States v. Grinnell Corp.* 384 U.S. 563, 570–71 (1966)] that monopolization under the Sherman Act has two components: "(i) possession of monopoly power in the relevant market, and (ii) the willful acquisition or maintenance of that power as distinguished from growth or development as a consequence of a superior product, business acumen, or historic accident."[8] The district court had found that Microsoft possesses monopoly power in the market for operating systems and that they have maintained this power not through competition on the merits but through unlawful means.

The first question the appellate court addressed is whether Microsoft in fact had monopoly power. It noted that monopoly power exists where a firm has the ability to raise prices above market levels or to exclude competition. "A firm is a monopolist," said the court, "if it can profitably raise prices substantially above the competitive level."[9] Because it is difficult to find direct proof of these circumstances, courts have developed a structural test. "Monopoly power," said the court, "may be inferred from a firm's possession of a dominant share of a relevant market that is protected by entry barriers."[10] The district court had found that Microsoft has a greater than 95 percent share of the operating system market and that its market was protected by a substantial entry barrier—the fact that software developers prefer to write for the Windows operating system because it has such market dominance and consumers prefer to use an operating system for which the most software is available. On this basis, the circuit court affirmed that Microsoft had monopoly power.[11]

Having concluded that Microsoft in fact had monopoly power, the circuit court turned to the second criterion for violation of the Sherman Act: use of anticompetitive or exclusionary conduct to maintain the monopoly position. The court noted that the development or acquisition of a monopoly as a consequence of a superior product, business acumen, or historic accident is not sufficient to constitute monopolization under the Sherman Act. There must be the use of anticompetitive means.[12]

In this connection, the district court found that Microsoft had engaged in a number of exclusionary acts to maintain its monopoly by preventing the effective distribution and use of products that might threaten its dominant position in operating systems. Here the appellate court noted that it is difficult to distinguish between vigorously pursued competition and illicit exclusion. "The challenge for an antitrust court," it said, "lies in stating a general rule for distinguishing between exclusionary acts, which reduce social welfare, and competitive acts, which increase it."[13]

In attempting to discern this line, the court pointed out that, to be illegal, monopolization must have an adverse effect on the competitive process, not just on competitors. For this proposition, the court quoted the Supreme Court in a 1993 case, *Spectrum*

Sports, Inc. v. McQuillan, "The [Sherman Act] directs itself not against conduct which is anticompetitive, even severely so, but against conduct which unfairly tends to destroy competition itself."[14] Nor is the intent behind the act important, said the court: "Evidence of the intent behind the conduct of a monopolist is relevant only to the extent it helps us understand the likely effect of the monopolist's conduct."[15]

As the circuit court explained, the courts have over time developed a complicated procedural path in this area. If a monopoly is found and exclusionary or anticompetitive acts are shown to maintain it, the monopolist may—in justification—show that the alleged anticompetitive or exclusionary acts are procompetitive. And after such a showing, if any, the trial court must weigh one against the other, determining whether the restriction on trade has, overall, a net pro- or anticompetitive effect.[16]

Using this analysis, and after considering Microsoft's arguments that its actions were procompetitive, the circuit court found that Microsoft had attempted to monopolize the operating system market by, among other things, (1) its restrictive licenses with original equipment manufacturers (which limited the ability of manufacturers to place icons for competing browsers on their proprietary desktops when they modified the standard Windows desktop), (2) its agreements with almost all Internet access providers, such as AOL (which provided that Microsoft would place their icons on its Windows desktop in exchange for exclusive promotion of Microsoft's browser), and (3) a threat against Intel (which was cooperating with Sun Microsystems on a platform for JAVA, a competitive program) that Microsoft would work with a competing chipmaker unless Intel abandoned the work with Sun.[17]

In each case, the appellate court found that Microsoft had no significant procompetitive justification for the anticompetitive or exclusionary acts alleged. In the absence of a procompetitive rationale for fundamentally anticompetitive or exclusionary acts, the court held that Microsoft had violated Section 2 of the Sherman Act by attempting to maintain its monopoly of personal computer operating systems.

Attempted Monopolization

The government also charged that Microsoft, in violation of Section 2 of the Sherman Act, had attempted to monopolize or gain a monopoly in the browser market by leveraging its monopoly in operating systems. The circuit court defined attempted monopolization as follows (quoting *Spectrum Sports*): "[A] plaintiff must prove (1) that the defendant has engaged in predatory or anticompetitive conduct with (2) a specific intent to monopolize and (3) a dangerous probability of achieving monopoly power."[18]

The court concluded that the government had not shown that there was a dangerous probability of monopolization, one of the three essential elements of the violation, and for that reason reversed the district court's finding of attempted monopolization. However, the court's view was not based on an analysis of what would be a dangerous probability of monopolization. The court simply found that the government had failed adequately to identify the relevant market or to demonstrate that substantial barriers to entry-protect that market. Without those elements, the court pointed out, it was not possible to prove a dangerous probability of monopolization.[19]

Thus, the court's conclusion was not that Microsoft had not attempted to monopolize the browser market but only that the government had failed to put into evidence the essential elements of the violation.

Tying

Finally, the government argued that Microsoft, by bundling its web browser with its operating system, had illegally tied the browser to the operating system in which it had a monopoly. Tying arrangements are generally considered per se unlawful—that is, wherever they are found, no extended factual inquiry into purpose or intent is necessary.[20] This is because the courts have found over time that tying, like price-fixing, could not be justified under any reasonable standard of conduct. The district court had found that Microsoft had tied the browser to its operating system by integrating the two and thus found a per se violation of Section 1 of the Sherman Act.

However, the circuit court held that the question of tying in this case should be reviewed under the so-called rule of reason. The Sherman Act prohibits any contract in restraint of trade, but as courts noted early on in Sherman Act litigation, all contracts restrain trade to some extent, and it could not have been the intention of Congress to forbid contracts in general. Accordingly, the courts developed a rule of reason in analyzing Sherman Act cases. Under this rule, all the facts of the alleged violation were evaluated to determine whether the defendant had violated the standards of conduct that Congress likely had in mind. In taking this position, the court believed that the special circumstances in the computer market and the unfamiliarity of the courts with the way the technology works could produce harm if the traditional tying analysis were inflexibly applied. Accordingly, the court remanded the case for additional trial activity and an assessment of the tying charge under the so-called rule of reason.[21]

Nevertheless, the court's analysis of what constitutes tying is instructive. The court found four elements to the tying violation: (1) the tying and tied goods must be two separate products, (2) the defendant has market power in the tying product, (3) the defendant affords consumers no choice but to purchase the tied product from the defendant, and (4) the tying arrangement forecloses a substantial volume of commerce.[22]

On the question of whether two goods are in fact separate products, the court examined existing precedent, which indicated that the tying good and the tied good were separate products if there existed a separate demand for each in competitive markets.[23] If competitive firms—that is, firms without market power—offered the goods separately, they should be considered separate products. However, the court was reluctant to conclude that the browser was a separate product on the basis of this analysis alone. For one thing, Microsoft had argued that integrating the browser into the operating system improved the functioning of both, and the court was concerned that applying a per se rule might stunt valuable innovation. For these reasons, the court drew no conclusion on the separate-products question but sent it back to the district court for resolution, insofar as possible, through additional proceedings at the trial level.[24]

The court then provided guidance for considering a tying claim under a rule-of-reason standard. First, the court said, the government must show that the integration of the browser and the operating system unreasonably restrained competition, an inquiry, said the court, into its "actual effect."[25] In addition, the government must show that Microsoft's conduct was, on balance, anticompetitive. As in the monopolization analysis, a defendant may demonstrate that the alleged anticompetitive conduct has a procompetitive effect, and the government has the burden of showing that the anticompetitive effects outweigh the procompetitive.[26] In particular, the trial court should attempt to determine whether the operating systems are in general sold with bundled browsers by other marketers of operating systems and, even if so, whether those companies would sell their browsers separately or offer a discount if the browser were not included in the operating system.[27]

The GSEs' Use of Automated Underwriting Systems

Although the circuit court was only able to conclude that Microsoft had violated the Sherman Act in one respect—its effort to maintain its monopoly in the Windows operating system—the court's analysis

shows that Microsoft escaped judgment on the attempted monopolization claim and the tying claim only because of special circumstances. In the case of the attempted monopolization claim, the
circuit court concluded that the government had failed to establish
two factual predicates that were essential to its argument. In the case
of the tying claim, the trial had not produced sufficient evidence on
certain technical matters concerning the computer software business
to give the appellate court confidence that the standards for illegal
tying had been met under a rule-of-reason analysis.

These problems are not likely to be present if the court's analysis,
as outlined above, were applied to the conduct of Fannie Mae and
Freddie Mac in their use of their respective automated underwriting
systems. Despite the fact that the AU systems are the products of
technological developments and are accessible over the Internet,
they do not depend for their competitive effect on their technological nature. They would have the same effect, and would be subject
to the same analysis, if they were simply a set of rules applied on a
case-by-case basis by employees in the GSEs' offices. In other words,
their effect is likely to be judged under the conventional tests applied
in antitrust law, all of which were carefully outlined by the circuit
court.

Nevertheless, as the Microsoft decision shows, antitrust law is
highly fact specific. Without a detailed inquiry at a trial, it is difficult
to differentiate between aggressively competitive conduct and exclusionary or anticompetitive action. There is a great deal that is still
unclear about how the GSEs use their AU systems, and for that reason it is not possible to draw firm conclusions about how a court
would analyze the GSEs' conduct in an antitrust context. However,
there is enough information to make a start on such an analysis from
the standpoint of a court using the circuit court's Microsoft decision
as its analytical framework.

Monopolization

The first question a court would face is whether Fannie and Freddie are competitors. Fannie and Freddie, together, account for almost 100 percent of the secondary market for conventional/conforming loans and about 70 percent of the secondary market for all residential mortgages. Of these totals, Fannie has about 60 percent and Freddie 40 percent in each market. If the two companies were truly competing, it would be difficult to charge them with monopolization, but all indications are that they are not competing.

In an analysis prepared for the Department of Housing and Urban Development in 1995 and published in 1996, Hermalin and Jaffee concluded, based on a painstaking review of a number of factors, including the GSEs' extraordinary returns on equity, that Fannie and Freddie were tacitly colluding. That is, they were not competing with one another, and the market they dominate—the secondary mortgage market—was not a competitive market.[28] That does not mean, of course, that Fannie and Freddie are acting unlawfully. Tacit collusion, unlike actual collusion, is not a violation of law. However, if Fannie and Freddie are tacitly colluding with respect to the use of their AU systems, and if that tacit collusion allows each of them to act like a monopolist with respect to those who use their respective AU systems, then they could be treated in antitrust analysis as though they were one company holding a monopoly in a single AU system. Of course, in a trial it might be determined that Fannie and Freddie are actively colluding. A conclusion of that kind, however, was beyond the scope of the Hermalin-Jaffee study.

The next question for a court would be whether the GSEs do in fact have a shared monopoly in the secondary mortgage market and in AU systems. Based on known facts, that is not a difficult question. As noted above, the GSEs are virtually the only purchasers of conventional/conforming mortgages and thus, together, have a duopsony in that market. Needless to say, for purposes of this analysis, there is no significant antitrust difference between or among a duopsony (two buyers), a duopoly (two sellers) and a shared monopoly.

Moreover, a February 1999 Morgan Stanley report on the two GSEs cites a survey showing that, in 1998, Fannie and Freddie together had 95 percent of the AU market—that is, the use of AU systems for the assessment of mortgage credit.[29] It is doubtful that this number has declined. A 95 percent penetration of a market, especially under the circumstances present in the secondary mortgage market, would on its face meet anyone's definition of a monopoly.

However, as discussed by the circuit court in *Microsoft*, mere domination of a market is not sufficient to find illegal monopolization. The monopolist must also have monopoly power, that is, the power to raise prices or exclude new entry by competitors. On the question of excluding new entry, that condition certainly exists in the secondary mortgage market where the GSEs hold exclusive federal charters together with government-granted advantages that provide them with lower interest rates and other advantages potential competitors cannot match. Accordingly, it will not be difficult for a court to find that the GSEs have a monopoly in the secondary mortgage market and that that monopoly in turn confers a monopoly in the AU market.

In addition, the GSEs appear to have the ability to raise prices for their AU systems without regard to actual costs or the prices that would be charged by their competition. Estimates of the cost of underwriting a mortgage loan on competitive AU systems are in the range of $15. According to sources in the mortgage lending industry, the GSEs' regular charges for the services of their AU systems are significantly higher than $15, indicating again that they have monopoly power in the AU market.

The circuit court also pointed out that holding a monopoly and having monopoly power to maintain it is not sufficient to find a violation of the Sherman Act. The monopolist must take exclusionary or anticompetitive acts to maintain the monopoly. Here there seems to be a great deal of published evidence that the GSEs have been engaging in such acts to maintain their monopoly. Those acts, which might be simply aggressive competition in a competitive market, assume a different character when taken by a monopolist in a noncompetitive market.

The GSEs have offered advantages to companies that agree to use their AU systems in preference to competitive systems. Advantages include (1) relief from representations and warranties that can result in a lender having to repurchase a loan from the GSEs, thus increasing the lender's risk,[30] (2) discounted AU fees[31], (3) provision of free or discounted additional software for users of their AU systems,[32] and (4) bundling of their AU systems with software that enables lenders to reduce the time and cost of obtaining credit reports, verification of assets, appraisals, and verification of income.[33] Finally, the GSEs refuse to accept any loans made under their popular low down payment loan programs that have not been run through their AU systems.[34]

Under the circuit court's analysis in *Microsoft*, all of those actions—and especially the last—would be regarded as exclusionary and anticompetitive, taken in an effort to maintain a monopoly. They are akin to Microsoft's actions in support of its Windows operating system monopoly that were found to have violated Section 2 of the Sherman Act.

The GSEs would, under the court's analysis, have an opportunity to show that their actions were in fact procompetitive, and a trial court would then weigh whether the procompetitive actions outweighed the anticompetitive. It is difficult to predict at this stage how such a balancing would turn out, but it is also difficult to discern what the GSEs might say in defense of their actions. Clearly, there is nothing explicitly procompetitive in what they have done, but the court might allow them to argue that their use of their proprietary

AU systems was needed to protect themselves against the possibility that they might be offered low quality mortgages. Although this is not strictly procompetitive, it is a reasonable strategy.

However, the GSEs would not be able to stop there. They would have to show that their proprietary systems were superior to others and that they could not reasonably be expected to accept mortgages that were underwritten by other AU systems. This, however, is likely to be a difficult standard to meet. It is doubtful that the GSEs have ever done a comprehensive analysis of the quality of competing AU systems. Indeed, at least one lender that had developed its own system asked Fannie Mae to run a test that would compare both systems. According to that lender, Fannie Mae refused. If, as this incident indicates, the GSEs have not bothered to test potentially competitive AU systems before rejecting them, it is doubtful that a court would accept their argument that they were required by sound business judgment to encourage or compel lenders to use the GSEs' proprietary AU systems.

Finally, the GSEs' AU systems are proprietary black boxes. It is not possible for a lender to know before a loan has been run through these systems whether it will be purchased by the GSEs. Under these circumstances, lenders, to be certain they are committing to a loan they can subsequently sell to Fannie or Freddie, must pay the cost of using the GSEs' AU systems. In this way, the GSEs' monopoly in the secondary market is being used to maintain and extend their monopoly in AU systems.

It is possible, of course, for the GSEs to make what might be called a Chicago School defense to the charge of monopolization of an adjacent market (automated underwriting) into which they are integrating. Such a defense would argue that if they indeed have a shared monopoly of the secondary mortgage market, they have no incentive to dominate or monopolize the AU market. This is because they can already extract monopoly profits from the secondary mortgage market and cannot earn any additional profits from integrating into an adjacent market. Thus, the GSEs might argue, the only reason they might want to integrate into an adjacent market is additional efficiencies, a procompetitive reason.

However, antitrust scholars have long recognized that this argument does not apply when the dominant firm's prices in the dominant market—in this case, the secondary mortgage market—are regulated.[35] Although the GSEs' prices are not formally regulated, they are, for political reasons, subject to some voluntary restraint. Under their statutory charters, the GSEs may not purchase mortgages that are larger than a principal amount set according to a statutory formula. Mortgages of this size or less are known as conventional/conforming mortgages. Mortgages in principal amounts larger than the statutorily established ceiling are referred to as jumbo mortgages and are bought and sold in a market in which the GSEs do not participate. Interest rates in the market for conventional/conforming mortgages are approximately 25 to 30 basis points lower than the rate for jumbo mortgages, and this difference is attributable to the GSEs passing through to homebuyers approximately two-thirds of the subsidy they receive from their implicit government support.

It is obvious that the GSEs must, for political reasons, keep rates in the conventional/conforming market lower than the rates in the jumbo market. Otherwise, there would be no justification for their existence. For this reason, it is unlikely that they can argue effectively that they are integrating into the AU market solely to achieve efficiencies. Because of the political constraints on their pricing in the secondary mortgage market for conventional/conforming loans, the GSEs still have the opportunity to extract additional monopoly profits from other adjacent markets.

It seems, therefore, that a strong argument could be made, following the circuit court's reasoning in the Microsoft case, that the GSEs have acted unlawfully to monopolize and to maintain and extend their monopoly of AU systems.

Attempted Monopolization

On technical grounds, the circuit court in *Microsoft* rejected the district court's finding that the company had attempted to monopolize the browser market. The government, in the court's view, had not defined the browser market or shown that there were barriers to the entry of competitors and thus could not show that there was a danger of monopolization. As a result, the court never discussed in detail the other elements of an attempt to monopolize: specific intent to monopolize and predatory or anticompetitive acts.

However, in its discussion of tying, the circuit court reviewed the relevant cases on the question of determining whether two different products represent separate products for purposes of a tying analysis, and this analysis seems applicable for determining whether AU systems represent a separate market from secondary mortgage market services. If this is the case, it would be possible to determine whether the GSEs are attempting to monopolize the market for AU systems. In its tying discussion, the circuit court concluded that two products were separate (and thus could represent separate markets) if consumers, given a choice, would purchase the tied product separately from the tying product. In the context of analyzing the GSEs' activities in connection with AU systems, the relevant question would be whether users of AU systems would purchase or license AU systems of their own if the GSEs were willing to accept the results of those systems as equivalent to the results obtained from the GSEs' own proprietary systems.

The answer to this question seems to be yes. Given the fact that the costs of using an AU system are significantly less than the prices charged by the GSEs and that many lenders have developed their own AU systems, it is likely that a purchase or licensing market would exist for AU systems if the GSEs would accept the results. Moreover, it is likely that a market for AU systems already exists in other credit-related activities, such as consumer or credit card lending, where the market is not distorted by the existence of two monopsonistic buyers. Thus, it should not be difficult to demonstrate that AU systems constitute both a product and a market separate from secondary market services and thus a market that the GSEs may be attempting to monopolize.

Attempt to monopolize is a violation of the Sherman Act separate from monopolization itself. If for any reason the GSEs are not found to have monopolized the AU market in violation of Section 2 of the Sherman Act or to have acted to maintain or extend their monopoly, it would still be possible to conclude they had attempted to monopolize the AU market, also under Section 2 of the Sherman Act.

Each of the actions cited above as anticompetitive or exclusionary could also be cited as evidence of an attempt to monopolize the AU market. They are each anticompetitive in nature and evince an intent to monopolize, meeting two of the three tests set out by the circuit court in *Microsoft*. Moreover, unlike the Microsoft case, there is no question concerning the danger of monopolization: The GSEs already hold an impregnable monopoly in the secondary mortgage market, and any service they require a lender to take from them could be an attempt to monopolize if the service is otherwise available from others.

Clearly, the most difficult element of proof in the context of showing an attempt to monopolize would be the showing of a specific intent. All the various communications among Microsoft officials that were used to demonstrate Microsoft's own intent are not available today in the case of the GSEs. They would have to be discovered in the files of the GSEs during the course of a litigation.

However, there are known acts of Franklin Raines, Fannie Mae's Chairman and Chief Executive Officer, that could be used as evidence of a specific intent to monopolize the AU market. In early March 2001, the *Wall Street Journal* reported that Mr. Raines had threatened three executives of large financial institutions—Wells

Fargo Bank, American International Group, and GE Capital Services—that Fannie would withdraw business from their companies if they remained active in FM Watch, a lobbying group that was attempting to convince Congress to limit the growth or range of activities of the GSEs.[36] One of the activities about which FM Watch had complained was the GSEs' attempt to monopolize AU systems.[37]

Fannie's action in this respect, an effort to cause the demise of a competitive group through threats from a monopolist, would be analogous to Microsoft's threat against Intel, which the circuit court found to have showed an anticompetitive or predatory intent. Accordingly, it could be considered in the case of the GSEs as evidence of a specific intent to monopolize. Again, the Chicago school argument discussed earlier might be applicable here. Because the GSEs have an incentive to seek profits in adjacent markets, they would not be able to argue persuasively that their entry into the AU market was effected for benign or procompetitive reasons.

In addition, other publicly known acts of the GSEs could be interpreted by a court as evidence of a specific intent to monopolize the AU market. In particular, the GSEs offered to evaluate, through their AU systems, loans that by law they are not permitted to buy or guarantee. A likely reason for this is to prevent the development of competing AU systems that might be established to evaluate loans GSEs cannot buy.

Accordingly, there seems to be ample reason to believe that, using the framework articulated by the circuit court in *Microsoft*, a court could find the GSEs are attempting to monopolize the market for AU systems.

A further question is whether the GSEs' activities amount to an attempt to monopolize related areas of the mortgage finance process. This is a far more speculative area, but facts as they develop over time could demonstrate that the GSEs are using their monopoly in AU systems or in the secondary market generally to drive out of the mortgage finance process unrelated or uncooperative companies that are engaged in offering title insurance, credit scoring, appraisal, the development of mortgage-related software, credit reporting, and mortgage insurance. In some cases, Fannie and Freddie have invested in companies engaged in these activities. In others, they appear only to have established contractual relationships that might involve cross-referral or other arrangements. The exact nature of these relationships is obscure, but in an antitrust case, discovery would permit their nature to be exposed and analyzed.

Discussions with lenders indicate that the GSEs may be well along in attempting to monopolize the appraisal market, especially the business of electronic appraisal. Traditional appraisal is done by a specialist in residential values who visits the property and estimates its value for the lender based on comparable homes and locations. However, there is now sufficient data on particular properties and locations to make it possible for the appraisal to be done electronically, through data processing, without a visit to the site or with only a viewing of the exterior of the property. In these cases, which are a substantial portion of all mortgage loans, the GSEs insist on the use of their own electronic appraisals and charge for this service, even though the electronic appraisals of lenders are as likely to be accurate and are less expensive for the lender and the homebuyer.

Indeed, circumstances in the electronic appraisal market bear a strong resemblance to what has already happened in the AU market. The GSEs' monopoly in the secondary mortgage market is being leveraged to give them control over other areas of the mortgage lending process.

Efforts on the part of the GSEs to integrate their AU systems with other services would provide evidence that Fannie and Freddie are attempting to monopolize products and services other than AU. In this connection, it is significant that Fannie Mae announced that all access to its AU system, after September 30, 2001, will be channeled through MornetPlus 2000, a proprietary Fannie Mae online system that links lenders, realtors, and others with providers of other services in the mortgage finance process, such as appraisal, credit reports, and title insurance.[38] That will provide Fannie with the opportunity to create and profit from significant competitive advantages granted to selected suppliers of those services. Because Fannie has a monopoly of the AU system that lenders need to be able to sell loans to Fannie, its selection of particular service providers, and not others, amounts to a direct suppression of competition.

It is important to recall in this connection, as the circuit court emphasized, that the Sherman Act is directed at the protection of competition, not competitors. The ability and willingness of the GSEs to favor certain companies over others, thereby excluding some companies in related fields from the competitive playing field, may amount to an attempt to monopolize under Section 2 of the Sherman Act or contracts in restraint of trade under Section 1.

Tying

Illegal tying occurs when a monopolized product or service is used as a lever to require a customer to purchase a product or service for which there would otherwise be a competitive market. The indications, outlined above, that the GSEs are requiring lenders to use the GSEs' AU systems and electronic appraisal systems is strong evidence of illegal tying. The tying product or service in this case would be the GSEs' monopoly in the secondary mortgage market, and the tied product or service would be the GSEs' AU and electronic appraisal systems. Alternatively, the tying product or service could be the AU system and the tied product or service the electronic appraisal system.

As explained by the circuit court in *Microsoft*, tying is normally a per se violation of the Sherman Act. However, in the Microsoft case, because of the technical nature of the tying and tied products, the court refused to affirm the district court's finding of a per se violation through tying. Instead, the court held that the issues associated with a tying violation should be reviewed under the rule of reason and remanded the case for further proceedings that would resolve some of the issues that seemed unclear.

There is no reason to treat the GSEs' use of their secondary market or AU monopoly as anything other than a standard case of possible tying. For reasons outlined above, there is no sense in which the GSEs' secondary market activities or AU systems present the difficult technical issues that compelled the circuit court to require a rule-of-reason test. Therefore, if tying can be found, under prevailing antitrust precedents it would be a per se violation of Section 1 of the Sherman Act.

Accordingly, it will be necessary only to show that the tying products or services—the GSEs' secondary mortgage market monopoly and/or their AU systems—and any tied products or services are in fact distinct products, that the GSEs have market power in the tying product or service, that consumers have no choice but to purchase the tied product or service, and that the tying arrangement forecloses a substantial amount of commerce.

There appears to be more than enough available data to support a strong case of tying against the GSEs with respect to their AU systems. It seems clear that the GSEs' secondary market monopoly has been used to require customers to use their AU systems and that this has foreclosed a substantial amount of commerce. That may also be true of electronic appraisals.

On the other hand, there is not yet sufficient data publicly available to make out a case of tying against the GSEs for all the other services—credit reports, mortgage insurance, title insurance, closing services, and the like—that they seem to be integrating with their AU systems. However, as the circuit court's *Microsoft* analysis becomes more widely known, it may be that victims of tying, who don't yet realize that the antitrust laws are applicable, will come forward to provide evidence of tying arrangements.

Conclusion

Even though the case was eventually settled, the D.C. Circuit Court's analysis in the Microsoft case provides a road map for analyzing the potential antitrust liabilities of the GSEs in three areas: efforts to maintain or extend their AU monopoly, attempts to monopolize the AU market, and tying of other services or products to their monopolized AU systems. Using this analytical framework, plus information already in the public domain, a strong case can be made that the GSEs have violated and are violating Section 2 of the Sherman Act by monopolizing and acting to maintain their monopoly of the AU market. A similarly strong case can be made that the GSEs are attempting to monopolize the AU market and the market for electronic appraisals. There also appears to be a strong case that the GSEs are illegally tying their AU and appraisal systems to their secondary market monopolies, which would be a per se violation of Section 1 of the Sherman Act. However, there is not enough information currently available to permit a conclusion that, in other than electronic appraisals, the GSEs are tying other goods or services to their AU systems. If such a case could be made, it would be a per se violation of Section 2 of the Sherman Act.

Notes

1. See *Microsoft Corporation v. U.S.*, 253 F.3d 34, and *U.S. v. Microsoft Corp.*, 87 F.Supp. 2d 30 (D.D.C. 2000).
2. Section 2 of the Sherman Act (15 U.S.C. Section 2) states the following:

Section 2. Monopolizing trade a felony; penalty

Every person who shall monopolize, or attempt to monopolize, or combine or conspire with any other person or persons, to monopolize any part of the trade or commerce among the several States, or with foreign nations, shall be deemed guilty of a felony, and, on conviction thereof, shall be punished by fine not exceeding $10,000,000 if a corporation, or, if any other person, $350,000, or by imprisonment not exceeding three years, or by both said punishments, in the discretion of the court.

3. Section 1 of the Sherman Act (15 U.S.C. Section 1) states

Section 1. Trusts, etc., in restraint of trade illegal; penalty

Every contract, combination in the form of trust or otherwise, or conspiracy, in restraint of trade or commerce among the several States, or with foreign nations, is declared to be illegal. Every person who shall make any contract or engage in any combination or conspiracy hereby declared to be illegal shall be deemed guilty of a felony, and, on conviction thereof, shall be punished by fine not exceeding $10,000,000 if a corporation, or, if any other person, $350,000, or by imprisonment not exceeding three years, or by both said punishments, in the discretion of the court.

4. Conventional/conforming mortgages are those that do not exceed in principal amount a statutory ceiling on the size of the mortgages the GSEs are permitted to buy. This so-called loan limit is reset each year by the Department of Housing and Urban Development based on average prices in the housing market.
5. Peter J. Wallison and Bert Ely, *Nationalizing Mortgage Risk: The Growth of Fannie Mae and Freddie Mac* (Washington, D.C.: AEI Press, 2000). Because of accounting problems at Freddie Mac, it is not currently possible to confirm the aggregate holdings of Fannie and Freddie at the end of 2003.
6. Morgan Stanley Dean Witter, Fannie Mae (FNM): *Technology Usage Ramping Fast; Look for Growing Fee Income*, February 1999, 1.
7. *Microsoft Corporation v. U.S.*, 253 F.3d 34.
8. Ibid., 50.
9. Ibid., 51.
10. Ibid.
11. Ibid, 54–57.
12. Ibid., 58.
13. Ibid.
14. *Spectrum Sports, Inc. v. McQuillan*, 506 U.S. 447, 458 (1993).
15. *Microsoft Corporation v. U.S.*, p. 59.
16. Ibid.
17. Ibid, 59–66, 67–72, and 74–79.
18. *Spectrum Sports, Inc. v. McQuillan*, 456; *Microsoft Corporation v. U.S.*, 80.

19. *Microsoft Corporation v. U.S.*, 80–83.
20. Ibid., 84.
21. Ibid., 94, 95–98.
22. Ibid., 86.
23. Ibid., 85–88.
24. Ibid., 94–95.
25. Ibid., 95.
26. Ibid.
27. Ibid., 97.
28. Benjamin E. Hermalin and Dwight M. Jaffe, "The Privatization of Fannie Mae and Freddie Mac: Implications for Mortgage Industry Structure," in *Studies on Privatizing Fannie Mae and Freddie Mac* (Department of Housing and Urban Affairs, 1994), 225–302.
29. Morgan Stanley Dean Witter, *Technology Usage Ramping Fast*, n. 4.
30. Statement of Donald Lange in *Bank Technology News*, November 1999; statement of Becky Poisson in *Mortgage Technology*, July 1998.
31. Report on the decision of St. Francis Capital to use the Fannie Mae AU system, *Milwaukee Business Journal*, 6 July 1998.
32. Fannie Mae press release, 1 February 1999.
33. *The Detroit News*, 13 October 1997; *Newsday*, 12 December 1997.
34. *Inside Mortgage Finance*, 8 May 1998.
35. See, for example, Robert H. Bork, *The Antitrust Paradox: A Policy at War with Itself* (New York: Basic Books, 1978), 376.
36. John R. Wilke and Patrick Barta, "Fannie Mae, Freddie Mac Accused of Making Threats Against Firms," *Wall Street Journal*, 8 March 2001.
37. See, for example, FM Watch, *GSE Mission Creep: The Threat to American Consumers*, March 2001, 3.
38. At http://www.fanniemae.com, see the discussion of Technology Tools & Applications/MornetPlus 2000.

Chapter 4

Anticompetitive Behavior in Postal Services

R. Richard Geddes

Anticompetitive behavior by government postal services is of particular interest for a number of reasons, including the following. First, postal services are a major industry in terms of both sales and employment throughout the world. Second, historically there has been considerable government involvement in almost every country's post. Most postal services are, or were at one time, government-owned monopolies. Third, many postal services perform a core, monopolized activity of letter delivery but face competition either on the fringes of their core activity or in other noncore activities, such as parcel and express mail delivery. Fourth, there has been extensive reform of many postal services around the world, which has led to increased commercialization and resulted in additional competition between government and private firms.[1]

In this chapter, I examine anticompetitive behavior by SOEs in the postal sector, both in the United States and internationally. Anticompetitive SOE behavior may lead to inefficient competition between government and private firms. Inefficient competition occurs when a higher-cost (less efficient) firm is able to use government-granted privileges and immunities rather than superior business skills, to drive a lower-cost (more efficient) firm from the market, deter its entry, or reduce its market share.[2]

I first examine the case of the U.S. Postal Service (USPS). I briefly review the special government-granted privileges, subsidies, and immunities enjoyed by the USPS. This review provides a template for understanding government-granted benefits enjoyed by other posts and also suggests the importance of thoroughly examining institutional details.

Following that, I present data consistent with anticompetitive behavior by the U.S. Postal Service. Finally, I review examples of anticompetitive behavior that have arisen in postal services internationally.

Privileges Enjoyed by a Government Postal Service: The Case of the USPS

Commentators often focus on legally enforced monopoly as the main source of economic value (or rents) with which to subsidize competitive activities. However, the USPS receives a variety of additional special dispensations that artificially improve its ability to compete with private firms. Special privileges enjoyed by the USPS can be grouped into two categories: (1) monopoly and suspension powers and (2) a set of special privileges and immunities stemming from government ownership or sponsorship. I first discuss monopoly and suspension powers.

The USPS retains several key monopoly powers: a monopoly over letter delivery, a mailbox monopoly, and the ability to suspend the delivery monopoly in certain cases. The delivery monopoly is probably the government-granted privilege that raises the greatest fear. It is a concern because the USPS provides both monopolized services, such as letter delivery, and competitive services, such as package and express mail, and can potentially use revenues from monopolized activities to cross subsidize competitive activities.

In the United States, the delivery monopoly is over letter mail. The Private Express Statutes prohibit the private carriage of "letters or packets," and the Postal Service defines a letter as "a message directed to a specific person or address and recorded in or on a tangible object."[3] The courts have accepted the Postal Service's broad test for a letter as, "the presence or absence of an address."[4]

The USPS's definition of a letter, adopted by the Postal Service in 1974, differs from earlier definitions and is much more expansive. Indeed, the Post Office and then the Postal Service has consistently expanded the scope of its monopoly over a 200-year period.[5] Such an expansive definition leads naturally to monopolization of materials not intuitively considered letters, such as bills and advertising matter. According to the Postal Service's definition, an addressed grocery store advertisement is a letter.

A substantial portion of USPS revenue comes from monopolized activities. In 2003, 56 percent of the Postal Service's revenues from mail were from monopolized first-class mail, while more than 26 percent were from partially monopolized Standard Mail (formerly third-class mail).[6]

Additionally, the postal delivery monopoly in the United States differs critically from other utility monopolies in that its scope is effectively defined by the Postal Service itself. Scholars have noted that unusual institutional arrangement. Gregory Sidak and Daniel Spulber have stated, "The result is unlike that in any other regulated industry: Because the Postal Service claims for itself the term 'letter,' which defines the extent of its monopoly, the monopolist has the power largely to define the scope of its own monopoly."[7]

The monopoly is well enforced. The USPS can conduct searches and seizures if it suspects citizens of contravening its monopoly. For example, in 1993, armed postal inspectors entered the headquarters of Equifax Inc. in Atlanta. The postal inspectors demanded to know if all the mail sent by Equifax through Federal Express was indeed extremely urgent, as mandated by the Postal Service's criteria for suspension of the Private Express Statutes. Equifax paid the Postal Service a fine of $30,000. The Postal Service reportedly collected $521,000 for similar fines from 21 mailers between 1991 and 1994.[8]

The fact that the USPS holds a well-enforced letter delivery monopoly over which it effectively defines the scope is significant for anticompetitive behavior. Competitors or potential competitors are likely to be reticent about entering, investing in, or expanding activities in which they fear competition from the USPS. Were the delivery monopoly more circumscribed, rivals would be less fearful of the redistribution of monopoly rents toward competitive activities.

The USPS in fact holds two distinct monopolies. The second is a statutory monopoly over the use of private mailboxes. The Criminal Code stipulates a fine if matter on which postage has not been paid is deposited in a mailbox.[9] The Postal Service's *Domestic Mail Manual* requires that mailboxes "shall be used exclusively for matter which bears postage."[10] Additionally, the *Domestic Mail Manual* specifies the size, shape, and dimensions of mailboxes.[11]

The United States is the only country that has a mailbox monopoly.[12] The Supreme Court, in *United States Postal Service v. Council of Greenburgh Civic Associations*, considered the constitutionality of the mailbox monopoly on free speech grounds. It came to the unsettling conclusion that postal customers must accept a monopoly over their own mailboxes in return for the privilege of being subjected to the Postal Service's monopoly over letter delivery. The court stated that "In effect, the postal customer, although he pays for the physical components of the 'authorized depository,' agrees to abide by the Postal Service's regulations in exchange for the Postal Service agreeing to deliver and pick up his mail."[13]

In addition to the delivery and mailbox monopolies, the USPS has the ability to selectively suspend the delivery monopoly in certain cases. Yale Law School professor George Priest has written, "In the 1973 Report the Governors announce for the first time that they possess and that they will exercise the authority to suspend the private express statutes at their discretion. No Postmaster General has ever claimed the power to repeal or to 'suspend' the private express statutes by administrative order. But the Governors have discovered an obscure postal regulation which will allow them, with sympathetic interpretation, to surrender bits and pieces of their exclusive grant in ways to preserve the substance of the monopoly."[14] Exceptions include the obvious, such as letters accompanying cargo and letters of the carrier (which, for example, encompass interoffice correspondence), but also include letters by special messenger as well as extremely urgent letters. The latter two exemptions allow for bicycle messengers and overnight delivery services. Although suspension of the delivery monopoly has allowed numerous businesses, such as Federal Express and DHL, to develop and thrive, it remains unclear whether Congress ever gave the Postal Service legal authority to suspend the postal monopoly.[15] Because it mitigates key potential opposition to the delivery monopoly, however, the ability to suspend the monopoly has been tolerated for decades.

The combination of an expansive definition of a letter, combined with the ability to selectively suspend the delivery monopoly, means that the USPS can effectively decide what falls under its monopoly. As James C. Miller observed, "Through its ability to define a 'letter,' the Postal Service is in the enviable position of being able to determine the extent of its own monopoly. While the service has 'suspended' its monopoly for certain letters (such as time-sensitive materials), it has also expanded its monopoly by defining letters to include bills, receipts, IBM cards, magnetic tapes, and other business documents. Typically, as new services such as express mail have developed, the Postal Service has first asserted that these services fall within its monopoly and then announced a suspension of the monopoly with respect to *some* aspects of the new service."[16]

The implications for anticompetitive behavior of the delivery and mailbox monopolies and the suspension ability are clear. The powers related to the postal monopoly are unlike those of other utility monopolies. The USPS is able to micromanage its monopoly power to garner the greatest economic rents while mitigating potential political opposition to the monopoly through the suspension power. Those shielded economic rents can be used to compete with private rivals not enjoying monopoly power.

The monopoly and suspension powers, however, are not the only government-granted privileges the USPS receives. There are a host of additional special USPS benefits, all of which can be used to artificially lower costs in activities where it faces competition.

It is exempt from taxation. Because it can borrow from the Federal Financing Bank, it enjoys an explicit government guarantee of its debt. It remains government owned and is thus exempt from paying investors an expected rate of return on their invested capital; that is, it benefits from captive equity.[17] It is not subject to a bankruptcy constraint. It has, at various times, received direct cash subsidies. It has the power of eminent domain. It is exempt from a host of costly government regulations including antitrust law and SEC disclosure requirements. It is immune from parking tickets for its vehicles and from paying for vehicle registrations. It does not have to apply for building permits or conform to local zoning regulations, etc. All of the government-granted benefits enumerated above are valuable and allow the USPS to artificially reduce its prices below those of more efficient rivals.

USPS Pricing and the Postal Reorganization Act of 1970

The above discussion indicates that the USPS has the ability to use numerous government-granted privileges and immunities to subsidize activities in which it faces competition. David Sappington and Gregory Sidak's discussion in Chapter 1 of this book suggests it has that incentive. But is there any indication that it actually does?

The Postal Reorganization Act of 1970 allows a test of the hypothesis that, when given the opportunity, an SOE will reduce prices in competitive activities and raise them in monopolized activities. Although the act appears to have tightened some constraints on the USPS, it greatly reduced the intensity of congressional oversight of pricing. Before the act, Congress itself set postal rates with the assistance of the Bureau of the Budget. Although that arrangement resulted in prolonged and sometimes acrimonious debate over relative rates, it nevertheless vested final authority for price setting in Congress and constrained the Post Office.[18]

To regulate prices, the act created the Postal Rate Commission whose five members are appointed by the president with advice and consent of the Senate.[19] The Postal Rate Commission was explicitly instructed to take the cost of providing specific classes of mail delivery into account in rate making through the requirement that "each class of mail or type of mail service bear direct and indirect costs attributable to that class or type plus that portion of all other costs of the Postal Service reasonably assignable to each class or type."[20]

That section of the act has been interpreted as an attempt by Congress to move away from using excessive first-class mail prices to subsidize other mail classes, which had been the case in the past. For example, the U.S. Court of Appeals for the District of Columbia Circuit in *National Association of Greeting Card Publishers v. United States Postal Service* stated that "Discrimination in postal ratemaking in favor of certain preferred classes of mail and to the great disadvantage of first class mail has long been part of our postal system. . . . In seeking postal reform through the 1970 Act it was a central and express aim of both Houses of Congress to end the abuses of this practice."[21]

However, Congress did not provide the Postal Rate Commission with adequate authority to carry out its mandate of cost-based rates. First, the commission must consider at least seven other criteria besides attributable costs when determining rates.[22] Second, the commission was not given authority to actually set postal rates, as

Congress had done, but merely to recommend rates to the USPS Board of Governors after a rate change request from the Postal Service.[23] A recommended change in a rate proposal is sent to the board for reconsideration, and the board can overrule the commission provided it is unanimous.[24] The board has twice used its authority to overrule the commission's recommended rates.

The third weakness is one of information, which has two dimensions. First, the commission lacks subpoena power. It must rely on testimony brought by participants in a rate hearing rather than demanding specific information from the USPS. Second, there are large information asymmetries between the Postal Service and all other parties.[25] This sometimes makes it difficult to obtain information relevant to avoiding cross subsidy.

Finally, the commission does not have the power to regulate the quality of postal services.[26] As an illustration, on July 25, 1990, the Postal Rate Commission formally advised the USPS of its opinion that it should not implement a plan to downgrade nationwide first class delivery standards.[27] On July 26, 1990, Postmaster General Anthony Frank responded in a letter stating that "After consideration of the opinion, we have concluded that it does not warrant changing our scheduled Saturday implementation of overnight standard changes. . . ." The Postal Service itself is thus able to determine critical variables, such as the number of deliveries per day or week and the speed of deliveries, giving it latitude for redistribution on that additional margin. Overall, the act effectively transferred control of Postal Service pricing from Congress to the USPS itself.[28] John Tierney has stated, "It hardly seems appropriate that a government agency enjoying a monopoly over certain of its services has the ultimate power to put into effect whatever rates it chooses."[29]

That may be somewhat too strong because USPS pricing is not entirely unconstrained. The commission's decision does force the board to be unanimous in overruling it. Additionally, Congress exercises oversight through committee hearings, and the Senate has input into board memberships.

However, the above institutional changes imply that pricing controls on the USPS were substantially weakened by the act. Given those changes and the behavior postulated by Sappington and Sidak in Chapter 1, the USPS would likely have increased prices in monopolized (i.e., low elasticity) classes of mail and reduced prices where it faced competition (i.e., high elasticity) after the act.

Examining price changes before and after the act across various mail classes can test that prediction. The three largest classes of mail are first-class mail, third-class mail [now called standard mail (A)], and fourth-class mail [now called standard mail (B)].[30] First-class is generally considered the most monopolized class because it is composed primarily of letters subject to the delivery monopoly. Third-class mail is comprised mostly of bulk advertising matter. Fourth-class mail is primarily parcels and bound printed matter.[31] Fourth-class mail faces intense competition from United Parcel Service, Roadway Package Service, and numerous trucking companies. Express mail, although small in terms of revenue, is also of interest because it faces considerable competition from private services including UPS Overnight and Federal Express. Express mail was not established as a separate class until October 9, 1977, so data prior to the act are not available.

Below, in figures 1 through 5, I show the real price—revenue per piece for each class—of first-class, fourth-class, and express mail over time. I also show the ratio of first class to fourth class and the ratio of first class to express mail.

Figure 1 displays the real price of first-class mail, the largest and most monopolized class. It indicates that a preact increase in first-class mail prices continued after the act was implemented in 1971 and that first-class prices leveled off around 1980. Figure 2 displays real fourth-class prices, which show a sustained downward trend after the act. The average real fourth-class price per piece was $2.28 in 1971 and reached a low of $1.21 in 1996, a decrease of 47 percent.

The final class of mail examined, express mail, is displayed in

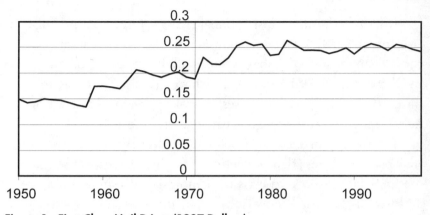

Figure 1. First-Class Mail Prices (1987 Dollars)

Figure 3. The act's effect on express mail prices cannot be examined explicitly because this mail class was created after the act's implementation in October 1977. Because this class faces intense competition, however, it is useful to examine its price behavior over time. Data for express mail prices from 1978 to the present show a pattern remarkably similar to the postact behavior of fourth-class mail. There was a decrease soon after inception, followed by a leveling off of prices.

Figure 4, showing the ratio of first- to fourth-class mail prices, is of particular interest. As expected, it displays a clear positive change

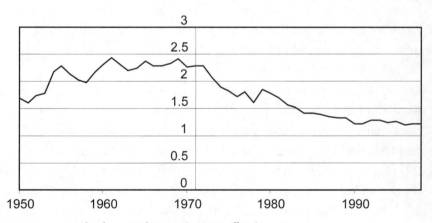

Figure 2. Fourth-Class Mail Prices (1987 Dollars)

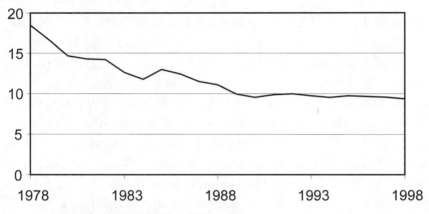

Figure 3. Real Express Mail Prices (1987 Dollars)

after the act was implemented in July 1971. There is no clear trend before the act. Figure 4 is also compelling because there are few alternative explanations with which it is consistent. As noted, court findings suggest that relative first-class prices were already too high before the act, so it is unlikely that Figure 4 reflects intentional adjustment of rates by the commission. First-class rates should have declined relative to other classes.

Moreover, it is unlikely that adjusting prices to cost would have taken 28 years were the commission endowed with sufficient power

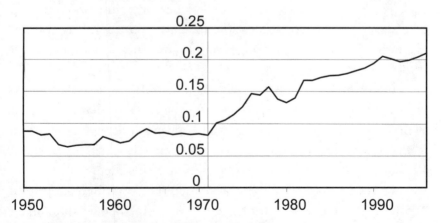

Figure 4. Ratio of First- to Fourth-Class Mail Prices

to control prices. Figure 4 is thus consistent with the USPS placing a greater burden on captive (low elasticity) customers relative to customers for whom they face competition; this is consistent with Sappington and Sidak's analysis. Referring to inverse elasticity pricing, postal scholar John Tierney noted, "Yet it appears that the Postal Service and the rate commission so far have done little to end the placing of an inappropriate share of the rate burden on first-class mail to cross-subsidize other classes. Although the appeals court disapproved of further use of the inverse elasticity rule, the Postal Service and the rate commission continue to implicitly apply it."[32]

Figure 4 is more suggestive of the slow extraction of monopoly rents to increasingly subsidize competitive package delivery, subject to remaining political constraints, than of successful realignment of post-act rates. Additionally, Figure 1 shows that the upward trend in real first-class prices leveled off in the mid-1980s. This implies that the increase in the ratio since then is due to declining real fourth-class prices, as shown in Figure 2, which suggests a large degree of diversion of resources aimed at reducing fourth-class prices.

Although the technology of mail delivery has changed substantially during this period, technological improvement is likely to have favored delivery of first-class letter mail rather than fourth-class packages.[33] The ratio would have then fallen over time under pricing consistent with the cost-allocation mandate in the act. It is also unlikely that technological change would have caused such an abrupt shift in slope in 1971.

Supporting evidence is provided by the ratio of first-class to express mail prices as shown in Figure 5. The trend in that ratio is not as pronounced as that in Figure 4 and appears to have leveled off in recent years but, as expected, is still decidedly positive. Between 1978 and 1990 the ratio increased by more than 65 percent.[34]

Figures 1 through 5 suggest that when the Postal Reorganization Act of 1970 reduced control over U.S. Postal Service pricing, it moved toward higher prices for monopolized relative to competitive mail classes. Data suggest that the act increased the ratio of first- to

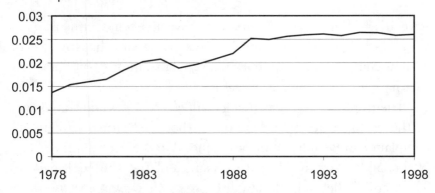

Figure 5. Ratio of First-Class to Express Mail Prices

fourth-class mail prices, and the ratio of first-class to express mail prices provides corroborative evidence.

Express mail and package delivery are not the only competitive activities into which the USPS has entered, however. The USPS has initiated many new activities outside its core area of delivering letters. It has expanded into selling mugs, T-shirts, phone cards, passport photos, and a variety of e-commerce services such as eBill Pay, NetPost Cardstore, and NetPost Certified Mail. It has done so without receiving the prior approval of the Postal Rate Commission.[35] The USPS has lost money on many of those services and in the process has weakened or driven private firms out of the market. The USPS is able to pass the losses from those services along to customers, who are captive to its delivery monopoly.

Although this chapter has presented only one test of the hypothesis, it is supportive of the conclusion that SOEs will cross subsidize activities where they face competition. Below, I review examples of anticompetitive behavior by postal services in other countries.

Examples of Anticompetitive Behavior in Postal Services in Other Countries

Given the extensive reforms in postal services that have been undertaken in other countries, it is not surprising that competition issues have arisen. Here I review issues that have arisen in Germany, Sweden, and Belgium. This is not intended to be an exhaustive list of current competition issues but rather to illustrate the types of issues that have arisen in the postal sector.

There are a variety of pending competition cases and complaints in the postal sector.[36] In addition to those in Germany, there are complaints in Belgium, Finland, France, Greece, Iceland, Italy, The Netherlands, Norway, Portugal, Spain, and the United Kingdom. The German, Belgian, and Swedish cases were chosen because there are several issues concerning each post and because of the amount of information available about them.

Deutsche Post

The experience with the German post office, Deutsche Post World Net, illustrates several anticompetitive issues that may arise under reform. Deutsche Post became an aggressive competitor as a result of the extensive postal reforms in Germany, particularly partial privatization. Deutsche Post retained various benefits after privatization, importantly including a delivery monopoly over letters in Germany.

There are three specific examples of Deutsche Post engaging in behavior that is potentially anticompetitive. The first involves incoming international mail, specifically mail from the United Kingdom. The second concerns its acquisition campaign. The third concerns the pricing of competitive services, specifically its parcel delivery service.

In 1998, the British Post Office filed a complaint with the European Commission. It alleged that Deutsche Post had intercepted, surcharged, and then delayed international mail from the United Kingdom arriving in Germany.[37] The dispute stemmed from a disagreement between the British Post and Deutsche Post about how to identify the sender of international mail. Deutsche Post asserted that all incoming international mail that had a reference to Germany (usually in the form of a German reply address) should be considered to have a German sender, irrespective of where the mail was produced or posted. Under the theory that such mail was circumvented domestic mail, Deutsche Post refused to deliver those letters unless the full domestic tariff applicable in Germany was paid. Delays of up to several weeks were common.

The European Commission investigated the issue and concluded that the mail did not have German senders. Instead, the mail was produced in Holland or Sweden or in the United Kingdom and was posted to Germany via the United Kingdom. The commission then initiated separate proceedings against Deutsche Post for abuse of its dominant position, on the grounds that it had interrupted the international flow of mail. The commission accused Deutsche Post of infringing upon the competition rules of the European Union by intercepting incoming cross-border mail, imposing surcharges, and delaying delivery. On July 25, 2001, the commission decided that Deutsche Post had abused its dominant position: "The Commission has adopted a decision pursuant to Article 82 of the EC Treaty finding that Deutsche Post has abused its dominant position on the German letter post market by intercepting, surcharging and delaying incoming international post which it erroneously classes as circumvented domestic mail (or 'A-B-A remail'). Deutsche Post's improper conduct warrants the imposition of a fine. However, in view of legal uncertainty at the time the infringement was committed, the Commission has decided to impose only a 'symbolic' fine of EU 1,000 on Deutsche Post."[38] The press release provides more detail: "The Commission found that Deutsche Post abused its dominant position in the German market for the delivery of international mail— thereby infringing Article 82 of the EC Treaty—in four ways. Deutsche Post *discriminated* between different customers and *refused to supply* its delivery service unless an unjustified surcharge was paid. The *price* charged for the service was *excessive* and the behaviour of Deutsche Post *limited the development* of the German market for the delivery of international mail and of the UK market for international mail bound for Germany."[39] Although the injured party in this case was another postal system, the episode suggests that a monopoly, partially government-owned firm will engage in anticompetitive behavior.

Deutsche Post has also embarked on an extensive campaign of mergers and acquisitions, including purchase of DHL, ASG, Danzas, Securicor, and Trans-o-Flex, among others. When Deutsche Post acquired a minority stake in DHL in 1998, competitors expressed concerns about that acquisition.

The European Commission was hopeful that requiring Deutsche Post to keep separate accounts and not discriminate against competitors would prevent it from doing so, stating,

> During the Commission's investigation, competitors expressed concern that Deutsche Post would be able to cross-subsidize DHL from its monopoly on postal services (i.e. for letters below a set weight and price) and to discriminate against competitors wishing to use Deutsche Post's network. Deutsche Post has therefore undertaken to refrain from cross-subsidizing DHL from its postal monopoly, to keep and publish separate accounts for its monopoly and non-monopoly activities, and not to discriminate against competitors. Publication of separate accounts will enable interested parties to ascertain whether Deutsche Post is fulfilling its undertakings. The Commission will also keep a close watch on Deutsche Post to ensure that these undertakings are being strictly complied with.[40]

With regard to its acquisition of ASG, competitors raised a different issue: that of utilization of government-granted economic rents to inefficiently acquire companies.[41] Deutsche Post also acquired Air Express International, a U.S. freight forwarder. Competitors were again concerned that Deutsche Post would use revenues from its mail delivery monopoly to undertake anticompetitive activities in the freight forwarding business.[42]

The European Commission found that concerns about those acquisitions were valid. It decided to initiate proceedings under Article 6(1)(c) of the merger control regulation on March 4, 1999.[43] The Bulletin states that "The Commission has serious doubts as to the compatibility of this planned acquisition with the common market since its investigations show that Trans-o-Flex has a significant presence in areas where Deutsche Post already has substantial market shares." The European Commission also found that Deutsche Post was cross subsidizing a number of foreign and domestic acquisitions with rents from its monopoly.

Despite those findings, in March 2000 the Court of First Instance found that the European Commission had failed to act sufficiently in response to a number of complaints regarding Deutsche Post.[44] The commission then undertook more formal proceedings. It focused on Deutsche Post's pricing of parcel delivery services for mail-order business. It found that, consistent with the concerns of competitors, Deutsche Post was indeed cross subsidizing parcel services. It was doing so by providing mail-order traders with significant discounts, known as fidelity rebates, if they would give all (or almost all) of their business to Deutsche Post. The commission found that Deutsche Post did not come close to covering its costs for mail-order parcel services but was instead using monopoly rents to subsidize certain services. It also found that Deutsche Post was charging its first-class customers an excessive amount to maintain the cross subsidy.

The commission concluded that Deutsche Post had abused its dominant position by granting rebates and by engaging in predatory pricing in the market for business parcel services.[45] Deutsche Post was then required to create for its business parcel service a separate legal entity (called Newco), with a system of transparent and market-based pricing between Deutsche Post and the new entity. The commission found that such a system would be a suitable safeguard against cross subsidy from Deutsche Post's monopoly. Deutsche Post was also fined for its behavior. In its press release, the European Commission stated that

> The European Commission has concluded its antitrust investigation into Deutsche Post AG (DPAG) with a decision finding that the German postal operator has abused its dominant position by granting fidelity rebates and engaging in predatory pricing in the market for business parcel services. As a result of the investigation, DPAG will create a separate legal entity for business parcel services. The system of transparent and market-based pricing between DPAG and the new entity for products and services they might provide to one another is a suitable safeguard for DPAG's competitors in business parcel deliveries that revenues from the monopoly in the letter market will not be used to finance such services. Furthermore, in light of the foreclosure that resulted from a long-standing scheme of fidelity rebates granted by DPAG to all major customers in the mail-order business, the Commission has imposed a fine of €24 million. This is the first formal Commission decision in the postal sector under Article 82 of the EC Treaty which prohibits abuses of a dominant position.[46]

This case is important not only for its large fine and the application of competition law to the postal sector but also for its solution: the separation of business entities and the requirement of market-based pricing.

Taken together, these examples suggest that Deutsche Post's conduct is a serious and legitimate concern for competition authorities. The tactics of an entirely government-owned postal service, Sweden Post, suggest that such anticompetitive concerns are not limited to private or partially private firms.

Sweden Post

Postal services in Sweden were deregulated on January 1, 1993. Sweden Post's legal monopoly effectively ended on that date. However,

Sweden Post maintained a de facto monopoly because its share of the postal market remained between 85 and 100 percent. Moreover, Sweden Post remained 100 percent government owned. Because of its government-owned status and its previous legally enforced monopoly, Sweden Post enjoyed substantial advantages over new entrants. Those advantages gave rise to several cases of anticompetitive behavior.

Privak was a new firm that entered the mail order distribution business in Sweden. It thus competed directly with Sweden Post. In response to that entry, Sweden Post entered into exclusive agreements, with customers obliging them to buy most or all of their mail-order distribution services from Sweden Post.[47] Sweden Post also offered various rebates and sales target arrangements that had the effect of creating loyalty to Sweden Post. The arrangements effectively excluded Privak from the market. It was found that those tactics inefficiently enhanced Sweden Post's market position and constituted an abuse of dominant position.[48]

Sweden Post also faced competition from CityMail and from Svensk Direkreklam AB. Competition was most intense in Stockholm, but CityMail also expanded into Malmo and Gothenburg. Sweden Post used an array of anticompetitive arrangements to maintain market share in the face of that competition. Those devices were designed to prevent the loss of customers to the new entrants.

The main instrument Sweden Post used to fend off competition was the geographic price differential.[49] That tactic allowed Sweden Post to set substantially lower prices in areas where it faced competition (that is, where elasticity of demand was high). For example, in Stockholm, where Sweden Post faced intense competition from CityMail, its price was about 30 percent lower than in other areas.[50]

Sweden Post, however, utilized a system of discounts and rebates that reduced the price even further. It constructed volume discounts that were specifically designed to confront competition from CityMail. When CityMail expanded into Malmo and Gothenburg, Sweden Post extended its Stockholm pricing system into those cities. It used tie-in agreements, exclusivity clauses, discriminatory discounts, and other strategies that were quickly condemned by the Swedish Competition Authority.[51] Despite legal condemnation, CityMail was driven into bankruptcy and was taken over by Sweden Post.

SDR competes with Sweden Post in the distribution of unaddressed letters within Sweden. It does not operate in rural areas, however, and had to rely on Sweden Post to distribute letters in those areas. SDR was thus in the unusual position of being both a competitor and a customer of Sweden Post.

The Swedish Competition Authority examined the situation and found that the price Sweden Post charged for distribution in rural areas was dependent on whether the customer in question also used Sweden Post for urban distribution.[52] As a result, SDR paid much more for its rural delivery service. The Swedish Competition Authority found the practice to be a violation of the Swedish Competition Act.

Belgian Post (De Post - La Poste)

Hays plc., a United Kingdom–based private postal operator, competes with the Belgian postal operator De Post - La Poste in providing business-to-business (B2B) mail services to insurance companies in Belgium. Hays has provided those services since 1982.

Hays filed a complaint with the European Commission against La Poste in April 2000 contending that La Poste was trying to eliminate its document exchange network by linking rate reductions in monopolized services to subscribership to La Poste's new B2B service.[53]

The commission investigated and found that the preferential tariffs Hays's insurance customers had enjoyed in sending general letter mail were unilaterally terminated by La Poste when those companies indicated they were not interested in the new B2B service offered by La Poste.[54] Moreover, La Poste allowed the termination of preferential rates to stand until the insurance companies subscribed to its B2B service, which they did on January 27, 2000.[55] The commission found that this misuse of La Poste's monopoly power made it impossible for Hays to compete on a level playing field with La Poste.

After a new management team was installed at La Poste, the company cooperated with the commission. It voluntarily abolished its practice by discontinuing its B2B mail service on June 27, 2001. The episode nevertheless illustrates the tendency of an SOE to behave in an anticompetitive manner.

Joint Ventures Involving European Posts

As noted earlier, there have been several joint ventures involving European posts. For example, Post Denmark, Finland Post, Norway Post, and Sweden Post created a joint venture in the express delivery market called Vasagatan 11 International AB. Joint ventures fall under competition regulations adopted by the European Commission. There are two basic provisions under which postal joint ventures may fall. They are Article 85(1) and 85(3) of the EC Treaty and the Merger Regulation. The Merger Regulation applies, in part, to any full-function joint venture with a community dimension. A joint venture is full-functioning if it has the required resources to perform, on a continuing basis, all the functions of an independent company.

Competition authorities have taken several steps to ensure that Vasagatan will not be inefficiently subsidized, and there are several elements of Vasagatan's organization that are relevant for policing anticompetitive behavior. First, Vasagatan will not engage in any services that are considered to fall under the posts' universal service obligations. Second, Vasagatan will be a stand-alone operation. That is, Vasagatan will operate at arm's length from its parents and will be free to subcontract with third parties to carry out deliveries but will have nonexclusive agreements with the posts for sales, marketing, and pick-up and delivery services.[56]

Summary and Conclusions

Private rivals do not enjoy the numerous benefits of government posts, which may include a monopoly in the reserved area of service, tax benefits, government-subsidized debt, freedom from paying equity investors an expected rate of return, exemption from social regulation, and other benefits. Because money is fungible, those privileges and immunities can be used to inefficiently compete with unsubsidized entrants. Inefficient competition occurs when a less efficient firm is able to use government-granted advantages, rather than superior business skills, to drive a more efficient firm from the market, deter its entry, or reduce its market share.

This chapter suggests that government postal firms have used a wide variety of tactics to inefficiently compete with rivals. These include fidelity rebates, distortionary pricing, interception of incoming international mail, discriminatory discounts, and others. Data on the U.S. Postal Service's reaction to the 1970 Postal Reorganization Act is also consistent with a government post behaving in an anticompetitive manner.

Various policies that have been used to address such anticompetitive behavior include the divestiture of competitive from monopolistic activities, accounting separation of competitive and monopolistic activities, creation of clear, market-based pricing for different business units, and the requirement that joint ventures function as stand-alone operations to avoid cross subsidies to competitive operations.

The examples of Deutsche Post and Sweden Post indicate that competition authorities must be resolute when confronting anticompetitive behavior by a government postal firm. In the case of both

CityMail and Deutsche Post's pricing of parcel delivery services, initial legal responses were inadequate to deter anticompetitive behavior.

A case currently before the Supreme Court, *United States Postal Service v. Flamingo Industries,* will determine whether or not the U.S. Postal Service is subject to the antitrust laws. Regardless of the decision in that case, the analysis in this chapter suggests that explicitly subjecting the USPS to the antitrust laws is an appropriate policy change.

Notes

1. For an overview of international postal reform, see Chapter 6 in Rick Geddes, *Saving the Mail: How to Solve the Problems of the U.S. Postal Service* (Washington, D.C.: AEI Press, 2003).
2. See Chapter 2 in this volume for a more detailed discussion of inefficient competition.
3. 39 C.F.R. § 310.1(a). In Europe, the delivery monopoly is more circumscribed, and Sweden, Finland, and New Zealand have completely eliminated their postal monopolies.
4. *Associated Third Class Mail Users v. United States Postal Service,* 600 F.2d 824, (830 D.C. Cir. 1979) (Wright, J.).
5. See James I. Campbell Jr., "The Postal Monopoly Law: A Historical Perspective," in *The Last Monopoly: Privatizing the Postal Service for the Information Age,* ed. Edward L. Hudgins (Washington, D.C.: Cato Institute, 1996), 18.
6. *U.S. Postal Service, 2002 Annual Report.* For a detailed discussion of the extent of the postal monopoly, see J. Gregory Sidak and Daniel F. Spulber, "The Nature and Extent of the Postal Monopoly," Chapter 2 in *Protecting Competition from the Postal Monopoloy* (Washington, D.C.: AEI Press, 1996). The monopoly power is a frequent topic of policy discussion. See, for example, Douglas K. Adie, *Monopoly Mail: Privatizing the U.S. Postal Service* (New Brunswick, N.J.: Transaction Publishers, 1989); Peter J. Ferrara, *Free the Mail: Ending the Postal Monopoly* (Washington, D.C.: Cato Institute, 1990); Edward L. Hudgins, *The Last Monopoly: Privatizing the Postal Service for the Information*

Age (Washington, D.C.: Cato Institute, 1996); and James C. Miller III, "End the Postal Monopoly," *Cato Journal* 5, no. 1 (1985): 149–56.

7. Sidak and Spulber, *Protecting Competition,* 12.

8. Sidak and Spulber, *Protecting Competition,* 31–32.

9. 18 U.S.C. § 1725.

10. *Domestic Mail Manual* § 151.2. There are no efficiency or equity arguments for the mailbox monopoly. Clearly, this monopoly is designed to preserve revenues, or economic rents, which can be used in anticompetitive ways.

11. Sidak and Spulber, *Protecting Competition,* 34.

12. Robert H. Cohen et al, "An Analysis of the Potential for Cream Skimming in the U.S. Residential Delivery Market," in *Emerging Competition in Postal and Delivery Services,* ed. Michael A. Crew and Paul R. Kleindorfer (Boston: Kluwer Academic Publishers, 1999), 143.

13. 453 U.S. (1981) at 128. See Sidak and Spulber, *Protecting Competition,* 35–37, for a detailed discussion of the case.

14. George L. Priest, "The History of the Postal Monopoly in the United States," *Journal of Law & Economics* 18 (1975): 79.

15. James I. Campbell Jr., in *An Introduction to the History of the Postal Monopoly Law in the United States,* mimeo, 27 June 1995, 29, wrote, "To mitigate opposition to its new definition of *letter,* the Postal Service also issued regulations which purported to 'suspend' the postal monopoly. These 'suspensions' created administrative exceptions from the postal monopoly for newspapers, magazines, checks (when sent between banks), data processing materials (under certain circumstances), urgent letters, international remail, etc. While the suspensions have prevented politically powerful mailers from petitioning for Congressional review of the postal monopoly, it appears clear that, as a matter of law, Congress has never authorized the Postal Service to suspend the postal monopoly. As statutory authority for these suspensions, the Postal Service cites an 1864 postal act. However, it is apparent from even a superficial reading of the legislative history of the act that this provision was never intended to confer authority to suspend the postal monopoly."

16. Miller III, "End the Postal Monopoly," 150. (In note 6 above.)

17. See Chapter 2 in this volume for a more detailed discussion of this concept.

18. John. T. Tierney, *Postal Reorganization: Managing the Public's Business*

(Boston: Auburn House, 1981), 104–7, provides a detailed description of the debate surrounding rate setting prior to reorganization.

19. 39 U.S.C. § 3601, 3624 (1970).
20. 39 U.S.C. § 3622 (b) (3).
21. *National Association of Greeting Card Publishers v. United States Postal Service*, 569 F.2d 570 (D.C. Cir. 1976).
22. These include a fair and equitable schedule, the value of the mail service actually provided, the effect of the rate increase upon the general public, and the simplicity of the structure, among others. See Tierney, *Postal Reorganization*, 111.
23. 39 U.S.C. § 3661 (b).
24. 39 U.S.C. § 3625 (a),(d).
25. Tierney, in *Postal Reorganization*, 115, states, "Though mail users and competitive delivery systems are investing huge sums of money in acquiring their own information and expertise, they find themselves at a disadvantage in facing the relatively information-rich Postal Service."
26. Letter of the Postmaster General to the Chairman of the Postal Rate Commission, 26 July 1990. Copy on file with the author. See also Sidak and Spulber, *Protecting Competition*, 50.
27. "Summary of Postal Rate Commission Advisory Opinion on First-Class Delivery Standards Realignment," N89-1, 25 July 1990. Copy on file with the author.
28. Scholars have noted this change. For example, see Sharon M. Oster, "The Failure of Postal Reform," in *Deregulation and Privatization in the United States, Hume Papers on Public Policy* 3, ed. Paul W. MacAvoy (Edinburgh: Edinburgh University Press, 1995), 114–15, who states, "In sum, the Act replaced the overly-meddlesome, highly politicized oversight of the postal organization by Congress with oversight by a board which is under almost no control at all, coupled with sporadic Congressional inquiry when particular interests are threatened!"
29. Tierney, *Postal Reorganization*, 210. Similarly, Sidak and Spulber, *Protecting Competition*, 100, stated, "Unfortunately, the current forms of public control of the Postal Service are ineffectual. In essence, the Postal Service is an unregulated monopolist that is constrained only in the sense that it is expedient for the enterprise not to show a profit."
30. The USPS instituted a new mail classification system in 1996. See *United States Postal Service, 1996 Annual Report*, 39–41.
31. *1996 Annual Report of the United States Postal Service*, 40–41.

32. Tierney, *Postal Reorganization*, 130.

33. Important advances have been in optical character recognition and sorting technology for letters, but packages must still frequently be physically handled. See Rick Geddes, "Technological Change and the Case for Government Intervention in Postal Service," in *The Half-Life of Policy Rationales: How New Technology Affects Old Policy Issues*, ed. Fred E. Foldvary and Daniel B. Klein (New York: New York University Press, 2003), 211–12.

34. Others have recognized the USPS subsidy to overnight services: "One widely recognized instance of charging different prices based upon the elasticity of demand is where the postal service has been charging a monopoly price for first class mail and then using the proceeds to subsidize the provision of overnight mail delivery which they suffer losses on. The recent increase in first class rates to 25 cents coincided with a simultaneous reduction in the government postal service's domestic overnight express mail charges to $8.75, despite the fact that the express mail service was already losing money at the higher price." John R. Lott Jr., "Predation by Public Enterprises," *Journal of Public Economics* 43 (1990), 246.

35. See *Petition of Consumer Action Requesting that the Commission Institute Proceedings to (1) Review the Jurisdictional Status of Fourteen Specified Services and (2) Establish Rules to Require a Full Accounting of the Costs and Revenues of Non-Jurisdictional Domestic Services*, Petition for Review of Unclassified Services, Before the Postal Rate Commission (15 October 2002).

36. See, for example, http://www.freefairpost.com/others/pending.htm (visited 25 April 2002).

37. "Commission Condemns Deutsche Post AG for Intercepting, Surcharging and Delaying Incoming International Mail," DN: IP/01/1068, 25 July 2001 (European Commission Press Release).

38. Bulletin EU 7/8-2001 (en): 1.3.44.

39. "Commission Condemns Deutsche Post AG for Intercepting, Surcharging and Delaying Incoming International Mail," DN: IP/01/1068, 25 July 2001 (European Commission Press Release). Emphasis in original.

40. See Bulletin EU 6-1998 (en): 1.3.48, available at http://europa.eu.int/abc/doc/off/bull/en/9806/p103048.htm.

41. The commission stated, "In the course of its investigation, the Com-

mission has, as in previous cases, received many complaints from private-sector competitors. They claim that Deutsche Post has financed its acquisitions with funds that have not been earned on the market, thus creating distortion of competition. The Commission will look into these problems in the light of the rules on State aid and public undertakings." Bulletin EU 7/8-1999 (en): 1.3.31.

42. Bulletin EU 1/2-2000 (en): 1.3.76.
43. See Bulletin EU 3-1999 (en): 1.3.32.
44. "Commission Initiates Proceedings Against Deutsche Post AG for Abuse of a Dominant Position," IP/00/919, Brussels, 8 August 2000.
45. "Antitrust Proceedings in the Postal Sector Result in Deutsche Post Separating Competitive Parcel Services from Letter Monopoly," IP01/419, European Commission, Brussels, 29 March 2001.
46. DN: IP/01/419, 20 March 2001 (European Commission Press Release).
47. Swedish Competition Authority, "Abuse of Dominance and Monopolization," OCDE/GD (96)131, Competition Policy Roundtables, Number 8, obtained from http://www1.oecd.org/daf/clp/Roundtables/abs13.htm (visited 9 February 2002).
48. Ibid.
49. See Erik Nerep, "Current Competition Law Issues in Regard to the De-(Re-) Regulation of the Swedish Postal Services Market—Especially the Problems of Defining the Relevant Market, and Establishing Price Discrimination and Predatory Pricing," Research Report, Stockholm School of Economics, October 1996.
50. Ibid., 4.
51. See James I. Campbell Jr., "The Global Postal Reform Movement," in *Mail @ the Millennium* (Washington, D.C.: Cato Institute, 2000), 172. Also see Swedish Competition Authority, "Abuse of Dominance and Monopolization," OCDE/GD(96)131, Competition Policy Roundtables, Number 8, obtained from http://www1.oecd.org/daf/clp/Round tables/abs13.htm (visited 9 February 2002), which states that the Swedish Competition Authority found this to be an abuse of dominant position.
52. Swedish Competition Authority, "Abuse of Dominance." (In note 51 above.)
53. "Antitrust Decision Against De Poste - La Poste Aims to Protect Competitive Postal Service from the Monopoly," EU Institutions Press Release (DN: IP/01/1738) 5 December 2001.

54. Ibid.

55. La Poste notified the insurance companies of the termination on 30 October 1998.

56. See Leskinen, Pekka, and Kent Karlsson, "Postal Joint Ventures and EC Competition Law Considerations: A Case Study Based on a Venture Between the Nordic PPOs," in *Emerging Competition in Postal and Delivery Services*, ed. Michael A Crew and Paul R. Kleindorfer (Boston: Kluwer Academic Publishers, 1999), 44.

Index